THE TRUTH IN THE
mirror

A GUIDE TO HEALTHY SELF-IMAGE

KARLA DOWNING

BEACON HILL PRESS

OF KANSAS CITY

THE TRUTH IN THE

mirror

A GUIDE TO HEALTHY SELF-IMAGE

KARLA DOWNING

BEACON HILL PRESS
OF KANSAS CITY

THE TRUTH IN THE
mirror

A GUIDE TO HEALTHY SELF-IMAGE

KARLA DOWNING

BEACON HILL PRESS
OF KANSAS CITY

ISBN-13: 978-0-8341-2270-3
ISBN-10: 0-8341-2270-7

Printed in the
United States of America

Cover Design: Chad A. Cherry
Interior Design: Sharon Page

Library of Congress Cataloging-in-Publication Data
Downing, Karla, 1958-
    The truth in the mirror : a guide to healthy self-image / Karla Downing.
        p. cm.
    ISBN-13: 978-0-8341-2270-3 (pbk.)
    ISBN-10: 0-8341-2270-7 (pbk.)
1. Self-perception—Religious aspects—Christianity. I. Title.

    BV4598.25.D69 2006
    248.4—dc22

                                                          2006014740

10 9 8 7 6 5 4 3 2 1

Contents

Acknowledgments

I gratefully acknowledge the following people:

Joyce Williams, who suggested I write a book on self-image when I met her at the Christian Booksellers Association show in 2004.

Bonnie Perry, for her positive response.

Judi Perry, for her expert editing and enthusiasm for the project.

Mom and Dad, for the use of their condo for my "writing getaways."

My husband and children, for their continued support and sacrifice while I write.

All those who have shaped my self-image.

Those who have taught me about self-image by being transparent and sharing their vulnerabilities with me. If you had not shared your experiences with me, I would have had only my own—and that isn't enough to write a book.

Those whose self-images I have damaged: May you find the willingness to forgive me for any and all harm I've done to you, and may you, through God's grace, let go of your damaged image and discover your real image.

The Lord, who reshaped my distorted self-image and is faithfully fulfilling His purpose for me.

The marketing team of Beacon Hill Press of Kansas City, for its support of the project.

Introduction

The image you have of yourself is important. Prov. 23:7 says, "As he thinks in his heart, so is he" (NKJV). Your self-image is who you think you are, and who you think you are directly influences every facet of your life. A low or poor self-image leads to lowly actions, and a good self-image leads to lofty actions. The image you hold of yourself is a product of your past experiences, your current interactions, and the way you perceive yourself. It is related to your self-worth, which is the value you place on yourself; and your self-esteem, which also includes the way you feel about yourself. If your self-image is distorted, you cannot accurately measure your abilities and will not be able to utilize the talents God has given you. Your self-image also greatly impacts your relationships with others.

How do you see yourself? Can you look at yourself in the mirror on the wall or in your mind and say, *His creation is good*?

When your image of yourself is *real*, you will be at peace with the person God has created you to be. Self-acceptance allows you to become all He intended without the weight of thinking more or less highly of yourself than you should. A real self-image also reveals truths to you about yourself and allows you to be transparent and open in your relationships with others.

What do you think the results might be of feeling good about yourself? What could you do with the emotional energy you now expend on berating yourself or comparing yourself to others? Probably a lot.

As you ponder the thoughts I share with you, I believe you can be set free from your past, useless comparisons to others, and the pain of inaccurate images others have placed on you. You will experience a new sense of satisfaction and pleasure in becoming *real*, not only by bearing the image of Christ but also by accepting that you are His unique creation, and you can live free from the distorted images you carry.

Are you ready to clean up your tarnished self-image and replace it with a real image built on truth?

1

self-image

AS HE THINKS IN HIS HEART,
SO IS HE.
—PROV. 23:7, NKJV

1

self-image

AS HE THINKS IN HIS HEART,
SO IS HE.
—PROV. 23:7, NKJV

When God created Adam and Eve, they were comfortable in their skin, literally and figuratively. Even though they were naked, they felt no shame or embarrassment before God or each other. They were transparent and real without fear of rejection (Gen. 2:25).

But things changed after they ate the forbidden fruit. Their eyes were opened, and they became uncomfortably self-aware and fearful. Instinctively, they knew to hide from God and from each other. In explaining the act of eating the forbidden fruit from the tree of the knowledge of good and evil, they projected their guilt, blaming their actions on others. Adam blamed Eve and God, telling God that it was the woman He gave him who made him eat it. Eve blamed the serpent. God knew their self-consciousness was the result of their sin (Gen. 3:1-13).

Adam and Eve had healthy, *real* self-images until the Fall. Up until that time they were unashamed, secure, cooperative, and complete. They didn't wonder if they were good enough; they felt accepted by God and each other.

After the Fall, they became ashamed, self-focused, blaming, competitive, and insecure. They were aware of their physical, emotional, and spiritual nakedness and their need to cover themselves. They were suddenly concerned with what the other person was thinking, and their relationship was based on power struggles, competition, and pain. They felt inadequate and guilty before God (Gen. 3:14-24).

Like Adam and Eve, we often feel inadequate and ashamed. We hide our true selves from others because of the fear of being known. Our relationships are imperfect and imbalanced. We don't see ourselves as we really are. Instead, "Now we see but a poor reflection as in a mirror" (1 Cor. 13:12). In the apostle Paul's day, mirrors weren't of the quality we have today. They were made of bronze rather than glass, and even the best ones reflected imperfect and unclear images. Paul reminds us that in our temporal and sinful state our perception is flawed, but that someday we will understand things fully. Part of that complete understanding will be in the way we see ourselves and others, our understanding of the value of each of us as God's creation, the wonder and perfection of our uniqueness, and the part each of us plays in God's big story. Although we won't have a perfectly real image of ourselves in this world, we can strive to gain a more correct image that is more closely aligned with the way God intended us to see ourselves.

Terms associated with self-image include *self-worth*, *self-esteem*, *self-confidence*, *self-examination*, *self-preservation*, and *self-respect*. Each of these describes an aspect of what you think, perceive, or feel about yourself. As we look at each one of these more closely, you'll see that feeling good about yourself isn't the same as being a "lover of self."

SELF-IMAGE

Your self-image began to form when you were born. It evolved to include awareness of your body, abilities, personality, looks, intelligence, feelings, values, and power. Your self-image continues to change throughout your life and is greatly influenced by your interactions and experiences.

An image is the representation of something that is supposed to be a likeness of the original. Image can be a mental perception or an actual object, such as a photograph or drawing. Your image of yourself is who you perceive yourself to be, who you present yourself to be to others, and who you think others perceive you to be. Self-image includes your assessment of yourself: your talents, personality, achievements, physical attributes, and behavior. It also includes a perception of your essence—or soul.

Your self-image may be accurate or inaccurate. It may be inflated, leading you to believe that you're more than you are; or it may be deflated, leading you to believe that you're less than you are. Your image might be damaged because of hurtful things others have said to you. Your self-image can be a reflection of society's values and standards to which you compare yourself. Your self-image may be stained by memories of past failures and regrets because of missed opportunities. Or it can be real—a reflection of the truth about who you really are—transparent and honest.

The image you hold of yourself is a product of your past experiences and current interactions with others, society's standards and values, and your beliefs about yourself. God's ideal is for you to project the image of Jesus Christ as well as the unique image He created you to bear.

SELF-WORTH

Your sense of self-worth is measured by the value you place on yourself. It is calculated by some type of measuring stick—your values, God's values, society's values, other people's values, or a combination of all these.

How do you measure your worth? Do you feel persons are worth more if they're productive, accomplished, beautiful, rich, a certain age, powerful, or popular? Are others worth less if they're uneducated, unattractive, handicapped, poor, or mentally ill? Do you value one race over another? Your first response is probably to answer, "Everyone is equally valuable, because God created all of us and loves us all the same." Do you really feel that way? Dig deeper. These subjective values are often subtle—and we all have them.

What is there about you that you're glad you possess? Looks, money, position, influence, intelligence, or talents? What do you not possess that you wish you had? What do you envy in others? When you compare yourself to others, what causes you to feel either inferior or superior? These are probably the measuring sticks you use to determine your worth and the worth of others.

The American culture has established itself in the work ethic. Americans value productivity and accomplishment. That's not wrong in and of itself, but it does spill over into the way we value ourselves. As a result of the work ethic, we may value accomplishment, success, and material worth more than we value virtues such as honesty, good character, and spiritual maturity.

The value we place on individuals is often determined by a set of criteria. Look at the following list, and identify which of these distinctives you use to determine worth.

- Physical appearance
- Education
- Ethnicity
- Intelligence
- Personality
- Money
- Possessions
- Occupation
- Goodness
- Popularity
- Fame
- Success

- Talents
- Relationships
- Productivity
- Achievement
- Influence, power, or who you know
- Approval from others
- Age

If you have trouble determining upon which of these you base your value, consider which of these if lost would cause you to feel bad about yourself and which ones you admire in others.

None are wrong to possess or pursue, but if you base your self-worth on anything you do or have, you risk compromising your sense of self-worth when the thing you believe makes you worthwhile is un-achievable or lost. If you determine your worth by your looks, you'll face a problem as you age and begin to lose your youthful beauty. If you determine your value by your actions, you'll feel less worthy when you fall short of your ideal. It's the same with achievements: When you fall short of what you consider significant or acceptable, or someone else does better than you, your self-worth may diminish.

Grant was on top of the world at age 32. He had made it: CEO of a big company, a six-figure salary, a beautiful home, and a Jaguar. Grant felt good about himself until he lost his job, his home, and a year later, his wife. His self-worth plummeted.

We also tend to judge our own worth by comparing ourselves to others. But worth is always subjective when based on a compari-son and causes you to feel either inferior or superior. To God, our worth is constant and unchangeable, and it's rooted in the fact that we're each His unique and valuable creation, valuable enough that He sent His Son to die for each of us (Rom. 5:8).

SELF-ESTEEM

The word "esteem" originates from a Latin word meaning "estimate." Self-esteem is a first cousin to self-worth. It has to do with the value you assign to yourself, but it also includes the feelings you have about yourself. One who has poor self-esteem is one who has a negative opinion of himself or herself. Conversely, a person with good self-esteem is considered to have a positive opinion of himself or herself. Some of the trademarks of positive self-esteem are acceptance, joy, contentment, security, and confidence. Negative self-esteem is associated with feelings of rejection, shame, self-loathing, embarrassment, self-pity, insecurity, and self-consciousness.

Self-esteem matters because the more inferior one feels, the more he or she tends to focus on self and what others are thinking. This interferes with the ability to be real in relationships and to be all God has created you to be. It also makes it difficult for you to truly love others as you love yourself (Matt. 22:39).

Low self-esteem is linked to feelings of self-pity and depression that keep you stuck and unable to see other options. It can even be used as an excuse to avoid making changes or to disobey God. Jonah experienced this. God told him to go to Nineveh to warn the Ninevites to repent. Jonah ran away and then decided to obey God after being swallowed by a large fish. He went to the Ninevites, they repented, and God forgave them. Then Jonah got depressed. He incorrectly mistook God's mercy to the Ninevites, who were Gentiles, to mean that Israel was no longer God's chosen people. He decided it wasn't worth living if the Israelites weren't special to God.

God reminded Jonah that He was a compassionate God toward everyone—He could care about the Ninevites, Israelites, and Jonah all at the same time. God doesn't want you to feel so badly about your life that you don't want to live. Jonah's misguided thoughts about himself and his situation led to feelings of low self-esteem, depression, and self-pity (Jonah 1—4).

Low self-esteem affects your relationship with God, because you find it difficult to believe that God loves and values you. Perfectionists hold unattainably high standards of behavior for themselves and transfer those feelings to God, believing He is constantly displeased with them. They can't accomplish enough to feel accepted. Shame-ridden people also have difficulty accepting forgiveness.

Nicky saw herself as a failure as a Christian, wife, and mother, and the more she dwelled on her shortcomings, the more depressed and anxious she became. She isolated herself from others, believing that no one wanted to be around her. She began to feel her husband didn't love her and withdrew from him. The more these feelings overtook her, the more she loathed herself. She became convinced that even God couldn't forgive or help her.

If you're convinced that others will reject you, you tend to push them away, reading rejection into benign actions and comments. This behavior may cause others to reject you because you're ultrasensitive and easily hurt or in need of continual reassurance. You may be suspicious of people who compliment or like you, wondering whether they have an ulterior motive, or you may refuse to accept compliments at all. You may also have weak boundaries and tolerate things that are destructive. Or you may be afraid to be yourself and as a result become a people-pleaser.

Persons with low self-esteem often see themselves as "all bad" or "all good," but this is an unbalanced self-concept. Those who perceive themselves as "all bad" have an overly guilty conscience and feel responsible for everything in their relationships—even the other person's behavior. Persons who present themselves as "all good" often have low self-esteem too. Their arrogance is actually a compensation for their internal feelings of inadequacy. None of us is all good or all bad. We have strengths and weaknesses. We do some good things and some not-so-good things. The ability to integrate the two and see yourself truthfully through God's grace, accepting yourself as you are and finding satisfaction in who He made you to be, is the key to feeling good about yourself.

SELF-EXAMINATION

If having good self-esteem means feeling good about ourselves, does that mean we shouldn't feel badly about sinning? The apostle Paul addressed this issue in Rom. 6. We're no longer under the law but under grace. Yet we shouldn't want to keep sinning, because we've died with Christ and have been raised to a new life. We no longer offer our bodies to sin, because we would then be allowing ourselves to be slaves to something from which we've been freed. Instead of using our bodies to sin, we should use them as instruments of righteousness for God.

Paul asks an important question: "What benefit did you reap at that time from the things you are now ashamed of? Those things result in death! But now that you have been set free from sin and have become slaves to God, the benefit you reap leads to holiness, and the result is eternal life" (Rom. 6:21-22). Christians won't want to sin for several reasons: It displeases God, whom we now serve and love; it causes problems in our lives; it hurts our witness; it isn't our primary nature any more; and we know that it will put us voluntarily back into bondage. Since we have another choice, the part of us that wants to choose what's good will feel remorseful when we choose what's wrong.

When you feel remorseful for wrongdoing, that remorse should serve as motivation to repent, not as a weapon with which to beat yourself. The remorse and repentance are meant to purify rather than pulverize and to uplift you rather than convince you that you're a perpetual loser. Constructive guilt spurs you toward doing better rather than keeping you stuck in your mistakes, feeling badly about yourself.

We're to examine ourselves regularly to see whether our actions are right (2 Cor. 13:5) and use the mirror of the Word to evaluate them (James 1:22-25). What we do is important. Self-introspection is a requirement of us not only as Christians but also as human beings who take responsibility for their actions and growth. Persons who cannot self-evaluate have all kinds of problems in life and relationships. If your self-evaluation is accurate, you will feel badly when you do wrong but not when you do right. The Holy Spirit convicts us of sin and leads us into truth (John 16:8). We are being purified and made holy (1 Pet. 1:15-16), and that purification process involves change. The difference between proper self-evaluation and low self-esteem is the conclusion you draw about yourself and what you do with the guilt.

Regina kept a checklist in her mind of all the things she did wrong, concluding that she was a poor example of Christianity. Because she felt like a hypocrite, she wouldn't witness to anyone about her faith.

After 13 months of sobriety, Steve gave in to the urge to have a drink. He felt so badly about himself that he stopped going to church and Bible study. He couldn't admit to the men or to God that he fell into his old habit once more. He felt completely defeated.

You should feel badly about doing wrong, but not about who you are. Who you are is a forgiven and redeemed precious child of God, made perfect in His righteousness.

SELF-PRESERVATION

Self-preservation isn't wrong; it's necessary and natural. God gave all living creatures instincts that guide them toward life-sustaining actions. You're wired to respond to danger at a primitive level. Your body is fashioned in a way that's self-preserving. You feel pain, which warns you to stop doing something that's potentially destructive. Your body repairs itself, fights diseases, and cleanses itself from toxins to prolong your life.

The apostle Paul assumed that we naturally care for our own bodies. He told husbands to love their wives as they nurtured their own bodies (Eph. 5:28-29). We're told that our bodies are the temples of the Holy Spirit and that we should take care of them accordingly (1 Cor. 6:19). An argument used against sexual sin is that we're sinning against our own bodies (1 Cor. 6:18). Taking care of our bodies includes our emotional, physical, mental, and spiritual selves.

Holly dressed plainly, didn't style her hair, didn't wear makeup, and didn't exercise. She told herself that God didn't want her to waste time and money on those things and that it wasn't "spiritual" to care about her looks. But beyond all her pious explanations, she simply didn't feel she was worth spending money or time on, and she didn't feel she could be pretty anyway.

Bobby pushed himself to the limit trying to make more money. To compensate for the stress, he drank more and more and ignored the physical signs of deteriorating health. Finally, he had to admit that he was pursuing self-worth and self-esteem through material possessions and achievements. Inside, he felt completely empty.

There are many harmful things we do, such as eating poorly, not exercising, living under high stress, engaging in various addictions, and choosing unhealthy relationships. Frequently those self-destructive actions originate from a poor self-image.

SELF-RESPECT

If you don't value yourself or feel positive toward yourself, you won't respect yourself. Your level of self-respect is revealed by how you take care of yourself and how you allow others to treat you.

My daughter Rachel had a high degree of self-respect. She knew how she wanted to be treated and requested that people do exactly that. She put a sign on her door that said, "I am Rachel. You will treat me with respect." She then wrote a long list of specifics such as "Knock before entering," and "Ask before you take my stuff."

As Rachel understood, self-respect often manifests itself in the boundaries we set with others. Christians sometimes confuse dying to their sin natures with dying to their right to set limits. "Dying to self" means living for Christ and not following our sin natures (Col. 3:3). We die to ourselves when we choose right over wrong and follow what God has asked us to do. That doesn't mean we can't stand up for ourselves in relationships or that others don't have the responsibility to treat us respectfully. If we truly love others, we'll do everything we can to promote righteousness in their lives (Rom. 13:10). Allowing them to mistreat us is hurting them. The second most important commandment is to love others as ourselves (Matt. 22:39). When we don't esteem and value ourselves, it's likely that we're not loving others as we should.

Another argument used as evidence that Christians don't have the right to ask for respect or have rights is that we're to "turn the other cheek" (see Matt. 5:38-39). The implication is that we should tolerate mistreatment willingly. This interpretation misses Jesus' intended meaning. He was actually explaining the correct application of the Old Testament law (Lev. 24:17-22) and New Testament practice to illustrate that God wants us to have an attitude of mercy and forgiveness rather than one of revenge. Old Testament law required judges to mete out the same punishment to the perpetrator that was done to the victim. But the Jews were taking it upon themselves to pay people back.

God never intended that. Jesus was illustrating that when people mistreat you, you can choose your response to them and that it doesn't have to be revenge. But this teaching doesn't prohibit you from standing up against mistreatment. Jesus responded to His own mistreatment during His trial by questioning the right of the high priest's official to slap Him, saying, "If I said something wrong . . . testify as to what is wrong. But if I spoke the truth, why did you strike me?" (John 18:23).

Another argument against rights is this: Christ didn't demand His rights—He laid down His life. That's true. Christ did lay down His rights and give up His life, but only because it served God's divine purpose. Prior to that appointed time, He protected himself and chose what He allowed others to do to Him. He controlled His sacrifice, not others. The apostle Paul laid down his rights but only when it promoted the gospel. He stood up for his rights as a Roman citizen and his right to be set free from unlawful custody (Acts 16:37; 22:23-

29). Later he was willing to lay down his life, but only when he knew it was God's specific plan (Phil. 1:19-26; Acts 20:22-24).

Allison was married to an angry and controlling husband. He frequently yelled at her, called her names, and refused to let her spend money or be involved in outside activities. Allison quietly submitted, believing that as a Christian she didn't have rights and that God would bless her loving obedience to her husband. She willingly bore the pain, degradation, loneliness, and hurt, believing it was the right thing to do.

Allison misunderstood the teachings about submission and rights. God doesn't want women to be mistreated or to be slaves to their husbands' demands, whims, and selfishness. All of us deserve respect in relationships. Both persons' needs and rights are important: "Each of you should look not only to your own interests, but also to the interests of others" (Phil. 2:4). There are selective times you should wisely, carefully, and purposefully lay down your rights, especially when it promotes the gospel. But you don't have to—and definitely shouldn't when it hurts the other person or harms you. You can help others make more healthful choices for themselves by asking that they treat you in a respectful way. But if you have low self-worth and low self-esteem, you probably don't respect yourself and tend to choose unhealthy relationships that devalue you. As a result, you hurt yourself and the other person.

SELF-CONFIDENCE

Self-confidence has to do with knowing you're capable. Self-confidence is related to a sense of competency. It's not sinful and is absolutely necessary to survive. If you have a poor self-image, you'll have low self-confidence, because your assessment of your abilities will be low.

Confidence is necessary for a person to function. Think of a toddler taking his or her first steps. The child is scared and at first holds on to a table. He or she then lets go, takes a step, and falls, then crawls back to the table, tries again, and successfully takes a few steps. The next time he or she takes a few more steps with a little more confidence. Each successful step results in more successful steps until the toddler has enough confidence to make it across the room. Eventually walking becomes natural, and the child doesn't even think about it. But when a new challenge comes—like stairs— the child will stop to reassess his or her ability, feeling less confident with this new hurdle. Eventually the toddler will gain confidence in this area too.

It's the same with any task. If you think you can't do it, you probably won't. A baseball pitcher who thinks, *I can't throw well,* probably won't throw strikes. A public speaker who is nervous and convinced he or she can't speak, probably won't communicate well. The antidote to this nervousness is to envision yourself succeeding at whatever you presently feel unable to accomplish, and as you succeed, build a track record that negates the fear. Not trying because of fear ensures that you'll continue to feel incapable. Most of the Israelites weren't able to enter the Promised Land because they didn't have confidence that they could defeat the people living there. Their lack of confidence in themselves and God resulted in the perception that they were incapable (Num. 13:31-33).

Confidence is related to competence, which is the ability to do a task well. We study and train to become competent in a vocation, profession, sport, hobby, or other talent. Competence is not sinful; neither is being confident that you can perform or succeed. The opposite of competence is incompetence. When you feel unsure of your ability, you'll either do more poorly or refuse to attempt the task. You won't make it in life if you feel incompetent at everything you do.

Women in her church kept telling Kacie she needed to be a small group Bible study leader, but she was afraid to commit because she didn't see herself as a leader. In spite of the fact that she was admired by many and was an effective encourager, she doubted herself. Kacie needed confidence. Finally she gave in to their requests, and as she began to lead, her confidence increased, and she began to grow by using her gifts and talents.

It is important to note that confidence and self-righteousness are not the same thing. Competence does not make you sinless or presentable to God. The apostle Paul knew his abilities and his credentials: He was circumcised, from the tribe of Benjamin, a Hebrew, a Pharisee, a zealous persecutor of the Church, and a faultless keeper of the law; but he knew that he must put his confidence in Christ for his salvation (Phil. 3:4-9). We can approach God's throne of grace with confidence, because He gives us grace and mercy through the blood of Jesus, not because of our righteousness (Heb. 4:16; 10:19).

We all have weaknesses as well as strengths. It's in our weakness that we must rely on God. Paul said that he preferred his weaknesses because they caused him to depend on the Lord. He was careful to boast in the things that glorified God rather than in his achievements (2 Cor. 12:9). Paul knew his strengths and what was easy for him. But he chose to focus on what brought him closer to the Lord.

Your abilities and competence ultimately come from God anyway (Deut. 8:17-18). Whether it's your intelligence, talents, gifts, appearance, or skills, it's God who made you the way you are and put you on the path to any successes you may have. He gets the glory, not you. But it's OK to feel good about what you do well and to admit the truth without feeling as though you're sinning by being proud.

FEELING GOOD VERSUS BEING A LOVER OF SELF

Is focusing on yourself unchristian? Is it wrong to spend time figuring out what you think, feel, and perceive about yourself? Is it wrong to have a positive self-image and self-esteem? Would it be better not to think about yourself at all and focus completely on God? Some Christians would answer yes to all those questions. But the truth is, you'll think about yourself because you're human, so it's necessary to analyze what you think and how it affects your life. It's the purpose of this book to help you think correctly about yourself, because if you don't, it negatively affects your life and your ability to serve God and others.

Christians sometimes feel it's wrong to have good self-esteem. William Backus and Marie Chapian explain it this way: "It *is* true that out of our old sinful selves no good thing can flow. It *is* true that without the Holy Spirit we can do nothing [good]. But it is *also* true that with the Holy Spirit at work within, *we* do the good" (*Telling Yourself the Truth* [Minneapolis: Bethany House Publishers, 1980], 99).

We don't leave our bodies when we get saved, and we still live our own lives. We're empowered to overcome sin through Christ, but we still *choose* to do what we do. It's possible to feel good about our choices, because we could also choose the other way.

Can we love ourselves too much? Of course. Having good self-esteem is not an excuse to be arrogant, proud, superior, or narcissistically self-indulged. Paul wrote to Timothy and described this type of person:

> People will be lovers of themselves, lovers of money, boastful, proud, abusive, disobedient to their parents, ungrateful, unholy, without love, unforgiving, slanderous, without self-control, brutal, not lovers of the good, treacherous, rash, conceited, lovers of pleasure rather than lovers of God —having a form of godliness but denying its power. Have nothing to do with them (*2 Tim. 3:2-5*).

A positive self-image is not an excuse for these attitudes.

A lover of self has little regard for others. A person with a good self-image is concerned with his or her own interests as well as the interests of others (Phil. 2:4). When we have a *real* self-image, we won't be selfish, self-seeking, egotistical, or self-centered but confident to truly serve. Jesus had a real self-image, and because of that, He was able to love selflessly without losing himself. Agape love requires us to love from a healthy self that's not self-seeking, proud, or boastful and doesn't do any harm to self or others (1 Cor. 13:4-7).

IT'S NOT REALLY ABOUT YOU

After all is said and done, this life isn't really all about you—it's all about God. When your self-image is healthy, you won't be burdened with inferiority, self-pity, low self-worth, low self-esteem, and low self-confidence, nor will you be self-focused or proud. In a sense, you'll "get over yourself." If your self-image is inaccurate, you'll hinder yourself and will be unproductive in serving the Lord, because that wrong image of self holds you back, holds you down, holds you captive, keeps you blind and confused, and causes you to be limited and self-focused. The self-image that results from low self-esteem and low self-worth usually causes increased self-consciousness and self-focus that prevents you from freely serving the Lord and others. Your healthy self-image lets you know that it isn't all about you, and, like Adam and Eve before the Fall, you'll be comfortable with who you are with the ability to be God-focused and other-focused.

QUESTIONS FOR REFLECTION

1. Describe the image you have of yourself.

2. From the list of things we tend to use to determine self-worth, identify the top five things you use.

3. Describe how your feelings about yourself affect your relationships with others.

4. How do you think your negative feelings about yourself prevent you from experiencing what God wants to do in your life?

5. When you realize you have done something wrong, how do you deal with it? How does recognizing the difference between the action and your worth as a person help you move forward?

6. How do you take care of yourself physically, emotionally, mentally, and spiritually? What else could you do to value the life God has given you?

7. Do you agree that Christians can ask for respect in relationships? Why or why not?

8. How do you respond to mistreatment in relationships?

9. Name some areas in which you feel confident and some in which you need more confidence.

10. Do you think it's wrong for Christians to have good self-esteem and self-worth? Why or why not?

2

DAMAGED

images

NOW WE SEE BUT A POOR REFLECTION
AS IN A MIRROR.
—1 COR. 13:12

EACH HEART KNOWS
ITS OWN BITTERNESS.
—PROV. 14:10

2

DAMAGED

images

NOW WE SEE BUT A POOR REFLECTION
AS IN A MIRROR.
—1 COR. 13:12

EACH HEART KNOWS
ITS OWN BITTERNESS.
—PROV. 14:10

We all have somewhat damaged self-images because of interactions with imperfect people in an imperfect world. Some of us are more damaged than others, but nonetheless, each of us is damaged to some extent. Anything that devalues you or causes you to feel less than competent inflicts damage and often results from the negative judgments of others that stick with you and define who you are. You're really somewhat dependent on others to help you figure out the *Who am I?* mystery, especially during childhood.

DEVELOPING A SELF

You were born without a sense of self. Infants perceive themselves as extensions of their mothers. Slowly, the awareness of self as a separate entity emerges. Language allows children to identify themselves with a name and describe themselves with simple phrases such as "Billy bad boy." "Billy good boy." Later they differentiate themselves from others with phrases such as "Billy boy, not girl." "Billy big boy. Tommy baby." A fairly complete sense of self as a separate entity emerges between two and three years of age.

Babies also learn about themselves from interaction with others. When they're held softly and gently, they feel good. When they're ignored or handled roughly, they feel badly. Babies need positive touch and a caring response to pain, hunger, and discomfort to feel loved and to develop a sense of self that says, "I exist. My needs matter."

Children are egocentric; they believe everything revolves around them. When those around them are angry, children see themselves as the cause of that anger. When those around them are happy, children feel good about themselves. Constant tension in the environment causes children to feel uncomfortable and insecure, because it feels as if the tension has something to do with them. Brad remembers concluding at age six that his daddy left the family because Brad didn't pick up his toys. No one told him that, but he felt responsible for taking care of his mother and sisters to make up for it. What a heavy weight for a child!

Body language also communicates information to children about themselves. Is the person smiling, laughing, making eye contact, moving toward rather than away, relaxed, and engaged? Or is the person frowning, disinterested, angry, and impatient? All these nonverbal signs communicate messages to children about themselves that are either positive or negative.

Overall, children need to know they're loved and valued.

THE IMPACT OF WORDS

"Reckless words pierce like a sword, but the tongue of the wise brings healing" (Prov. 12:18). Words carry messages that heavily impact self-image. We all need input from others on how we're doing and who we are, which is why even a lack of words and affirmation is received as negative feedback. Children who don't hear words that communicate "I love you, and you're special" don't feel valued. Any feedback or lack of feedback that's devaluing, hurtful, or limiting can be damaging. Imagine the impact on a child's emerging sense of self from these messages:

- You never do anything right.
- You ruined my life.
- Why can't you be more like your sister/brother?
- You're a bad boy/girl.

Compare those statements to these:

- You're my special boy/girl.

- You're a blessing.
- I'm so proud of you.
- You're God's special creation.

Children see their parents as powerful and wise. They can't discern the difference between truth and lies; they can't reason that their parents' messages are distorted. Instead, they receive the messages as truth and integrate those messages into their self-images.

We're affected by the things that were said to us; but we do have some control over the degree to which we let those messages define our lives. When you hear something said about you such as "You're stupid" or "You're just like your dad," you might make an inaccurate judgment about yourself such as "I'm unlovable." "I'll never measure up." "I need to be different to be liked." It's the conclusions you draw that damage your image even more than the things that are said.

Sue's dad continually compared her to her sister, saying "Why can't you be more like her?" Sue reminded her dad of his ex-wife, her mother, against whom he harbored anger. He repeatedly told Sue that she would turn out to be "no good like your mom." In spite of understanding that her dad had problems of his own, Sue couldn't shake the sense of worthlessness. She concluded that she was like her mom and that it was her fault that her dad didn't love her. If, instead, Sue could see that her dad's distorted perceptions led to his inaccurate messages about her, she could have chosen not to accept his conclusions.

THE IMPACT OF LABELS

God named Adam and Eve after He created them, and He instructed Adam to name the animals (Gen. 2:19). God often used names to shape self-images. He changed Abram's name to Abraham (Gen. 17:3-5), which means "the father of many." God was telling him that He would fulfill His promise to make him the father of a great nation. He changed Sarai to Sarah, stressing that she, too, would be the mother of many people (vv. 15-16). He wanted Abraham and Sarah to have new self-images that paralleled His plan for them. Jesus' names are reflective of His image: "Wonderful Counselor, Mighty God, Everlasting Father, Prince of Peace" (Isa. 9:6). Jesus used labels to pierce the calloused hearts of the Pharisees, calling them hypocrites (Matt. 23:13-29), snakes and a brood of vipers (v. 33), and compared them to whitewashed tombs (v. 27).

Labels have a huge impact, because they describe and make value judgments. Think back to your school days to the labels kids used: "Dummy," "Retard," "Baby," "Sissy," "Bird Legs," "Four-eyes," "Clumsy," "Fatso," "Nerd." The labeled child is often unfairly defined by one characteristic. Many adults carry wounds from childhood rejection by peers. Everyone has a primary need to belong and to be accepted. Were you labeled and shunned by peers? Does that memory bring back a vivid sensation of the emotions you felt at the time—even though it was long ago?

Labels shape self-image. They're especially damaging when they describe a defect—like the child with a learning disability who's labeled "stupid," or the small, nonathletic boy who's labeled "clumsy."

For me, junior high school was a vulnerable time, and I was deeply affected by what some of my peers thought about me. I was a good student and some kids made fun of me for being smart and called me "Goody-good" and "Brains." I began to see "smart" as bad, so I stopped getting good grades. For others it was more serious. Gail was laughed at by the other girls and boys who made fun of her clothes and hair. Guy had a severe stutter that the kids imitated. And Justine was labeled "Scarface," because she had a large burn scar from a childhood accident.

Labels are judgments based on the standards and interpretations of others; they're not necessarily accurate. They may be related to cultural norms and biases, peer pressure, one's own damaged self-image, or personal values. All are damaging if you use them to measure your self-worth and absorb them into your self-image.

THE IMPACT OF PRIMARY MESSAGES

Your parents and other significant people in your childhood communicated primary messages to you—positive or negative, encouraging or discouraging, helpful or hurtful. These messages may have come from your parents' damaged self-images. Children are unable to judge whether or not the messages are healthful or unhealthful, so they incorporate them into their self-images and carry them into adulthood. Here are some examples:

- Work hard and succeed—then you'll be someone.
- Be perfect.
- You can do anything.
- You'll never amount to anything.
- Keep your problems to yourself.
- Always be happy, and don't show any bad emotions.
- Don't complain. Be grateful for whatever you have.
- Life is uncertain. Be careful, and don't take risks.

Can you see how each of these messages would impact a child's self-image and view of the world? For instance, when children are told to be good, and when they receive positive feedback only when they're perfect, they feel positive about themselves only when doing something good; when doing something less than perfect, the feeling about self is negative, because they judge themselves by that same standard. The message "You're smart and capable" will translate into a positive and confident self-image. The child who feels unaccepted by his or her own parents may conclude, "If I'm not good enough for my parents to love me, nobody else will either."

Brenda remembers feeling that her mom didn't love her. She tried to get her approval by being a good student and accomplishing things, but her mom always wanted more. As an adult, no matter what Brenda accomplishes, she feels like a failure, because she's struggling with a damaged image that tells her that she must perform to feel good about herself. She wasn't able to please her unrealistic mother, and now she can't please her own unrealistic standards. Her damaged image says, "I'll always fall short."

Try to identify the primary messages you received as a child. How did they shape your self-image?

THE IMPACT OF CONFLICTING MESSAGES

When two important people give you conflicting messages, it causes internal struggle. You don't know who to believe or who to please. Here are some examples of conflicting messages:

- Dad says, "You're pretty." Mom says, "It's not good to be pretty, because men will only want you for your looks."
- Dad says, "Boys don't cry." Mom says, "Boys should be sensitive."
- Dad says, "Work hard." Mom says, "Play and have fun."

Messages also conflict when the words don't match the underlying meaning, tone, body language, or action. Consider these examples:

- "I love you" [but I'm harming you at the same time with abuse].
- "You can go play. Mom will be OK alone—again," leaving the child with guilt about choosing to leave Mom.
- "I love you—leave me alone," says I don't really want to be with you, which leaves a child confused over what love is and whether or not he or she is valued.

Conflicting messages from your parents cause a split in your self-image, because to please one is to displease the other. No matter what you do, you feel bad about yourself.

THE IMPACT OF EXPECTATIONS

Adults label children with descriptions that shape their self-images. When a parent describes a child as difficult, demanding, negative, fragile, or manipulative, the child sees himself or herself as being that way. He or she will develop a self-image that says, "I'm a difficult child." "I'm demanding." "I'm fragile." The child then begins to behave in a way that fits that particular image. This does not mean you can never speak the truth about a child's personality or actions, but be very careful of how you talk about the child in his or her presence, and watch how you define behavior. When you remember that we're what we *think* we are, you more easily realize that your words have an impact in defining who a child is.

Because we're partially dependent on the feedback of others in developing our self-images, we attempt to be what we think others see us as. If others see you as a loser, you're probably more inclined to make choices and decisions that reinforce that notion. When something unfortunate happens, you see it as reinforcing the damaged image that you truly are a loser. In contrast, if you see yourself as a winner, you'll make choices that reinforce that view and will tolerate disappointment without coming to the conclusion that you're a loser.

THE IMPACT OF INCOMPETENCE

Self-esteem is partially built on the feeling of being competent. Persons with damaged images view themselves as inadequate in one or more areas and sometimes have an overall assessment of themselves as completely inadequate.

Moses felt incompetent in his ability to speak to the people when God asked him to lead the Israelites out of Egypt, but God must have felt he could do it, or He wouldn't have chosen him. To accommodate Moses' perceived inadequacy, God allowed Moses' brother Aaron to do his speaking (Exod. 4:10-16).

In what areas do you feel competent rather than incompetent? Do you feel and act the same way when you feel confident as when you're insecure? I doubt it. Your self-image affects how you act. Unless you're really good at faking it, you'll act differently in those situations. Self-confidence is about trusting yourself to be capable. If your image is damaged, you won't see yourself as capable, even though you might be. As a result, you'll be less likely to attempt new things.

When I was a kid, I felt incapable of doing sports. I hated physical education classes to the point of refusing to go to that class in high school. I don't know why I felt so inept, but I did. Today I'm actually fairly athletic and enjoy sports. I don't think I would have been a star athlete, but I could have participated. My feeling of inadequacy limited me.

Parents can plant a sense of incompetence in their children by refusing to allow them to do difficult things that will allow them to learn from their mistakes. Both the overly protective and overly critical parent sends a message to the child that he or she is incapable. Children need to be given increasing amounts of control, choice, and opportunity to build mastery of themselves and the world. Inappropriate expectations, such as expecting a three-year-old to keep his or her room perfectly clean or never cry will damage the child's self-image—because the expectation can't be met.

THE IMPACT OF ABUSE

Abuse can be verbal, emotional, spiritual, physical, or sexual. Underlying abuse is the need of the abuser to control, manipulate, tear down, or hurt. All abuse leaves deep wounds in the recipient's self-image. All result in the abused asking, "What did I do to deserve being treated this way?" and "What's wrong with me?" rather than "What's wrong with this person to treat me this way?" Abuse is the opposite of love, which should do no harm (Rom. 13:10). The effects can range from low self-esteem, unhappiness, loss of self-respect, dissatisfaction with the relationship, to the complete disintegration of personal worth and one's self-image. Eventually, the abused usually concludes that the treatment is deserved and surrenders to it.

Verbal and emotional abuse is any communication or act designed to attack or tear down the recipient. Emotional abuse often accompanies other forms of abuse and includes blaming, withdrawal of approval, withdrawal of financial support or material needs, silent treatments, threats, blackmail, bullying, and manipulation. Verbal abuse includes criticizing, calling the person names, ridiculing the person, and threatening him or her. Any form of verbal or emotional abuse results in low self-esteem and low self-worth. If you've suffered from this form of abuse, your self-image has been affected, and you may find yourself doubting yourself whenever someone questions or disagrees with you.

Physical abuse is any type of touch that's not given in love. It ranges from occasional milder forms such as slapping or shoving in an argument to battering where the abuser periodically beats the abused severely. All touch not given in love tears down the self-image of the recipient.

Spiritual abuse is the misuse of spiritual authority and power and involves using the Bible or one's position to control, intimidate, punish, manipulate, or tear down. It might be a father who threatens that God will punish a child who misbehaves, or a father who is a tyrant and justifies it because the Bible makes him the head of his home, or a husband who uses biblical authority over his wife to demand obedience and prevent her from having an opinion and disregards her feelings. Pastors have authority over their flock but can misuse it by lording it over people or by having a judgmental and condemning attitude (1 Pet. 5:2-3).

If you were sexually abused as a child, you carry a wounded self-image and have probably struggled with feeling dirty, worthless, and shameful. You may react to that shame either by becoming sexually promiscuous or by isolating and refusing to have intimate relationships. It's particularly difficult to come to terms with the fact that in some ways you may have enjoyed it. God created our bodies to respond sexually, and even when the sex is manipulated or coerced, our bodies are still capable of experiencing the pleasurable feelings associated with sexual stimulation. The manipulation and sophistication of molesters is overpowering to a child who is powerless to say no, especially when threats and coercion are used. It may feel as though you willingly agreed to the encounters when, in fact, you were being controlled and manipulated. The fear of others finding out was tied to the shame you felt. Then, if people found out and reacted in a way that reinforced your shame, they further perpetuated the image that you had done something shameful.

This happened to King David's daughter, Tamar (2 Sam. 13). Her brother, Amnon, raped her and then despised her. When her other brother, Absalom, found out, he advised her to be quiet and had her live in his home as a desolate and shamed woman. When her father, King David, found out, he was angry but did nothing about it. No one confronted Amnon nor comforted Tamar. She unfairly bore the shame of his sin.

THE IMPACT OF MODELS

Our parents' views of themselves also affect our self-images. A mother who is comfortable with her femininity is a model for a daughter feeling good about being a girl. Likewise, a father who is comfortable with his masculinity is a good model for his son. The messages and stereotypes that the mother and father hold about female and male roles further define their children's self-images. Consider some of these messages:

- Boys don't cry or show weakness.
- Women should be content with being mothers and wives and not want anything more in life.
- A woman should be weaker than her man.

- Men work outside the home; women work in the home.
- Nice girls don't like sex.
- Boys will be boys and have sex with anyone they can.

Just as those messages shape the self-image of children, so do the parents' reaction to their children's emerging sexuality, especially their daughters. The underlying fear of their daughters growing up and being attractive to the opposite sex and possibly engaging in sexual activities causes some parents to react in a negative way to their appearance by saying things like "You look like a slut," "You just want boys to notice you," "You're embarrassing me." You can address inappropriate dress in a more productive way, such as, "I don't think that's appropriate. Please change." By commenting on the look without attacking the child, you avoid damaging his or her self-image.

Your parents' example also affects your relationship with God and other people. If your father was harsh, absent, or critical, you may have difficulty feeling loved and accepted by God the Father. If one or both of your parents is mistreated as a result of a gender role, you'll especially struggle with your self-image if you're of the same gender.

Katie's dad was withdrawn and focused on his work. If he did interact with her, he was harsh and abrupt. He was also disrespectful and verbally abusive to her mother. As an adult, Katie struggles with accepting God's love for her. It's easier for her to relate to Jesus, who was kind and loving and willing to die for her. God remains distant, judgmental, and harsh. She picks men who are unavailable and verbally abusive. She sees herself as another woman deserving to be treated badly by men.

Parents with poor self-esteem see their children's successes or failures as a reflection of their own worth. Parents might push a child hard to succeed in an area the parent was deficient in, or they may do the opposite and actually compete with or feel jealous of their child's abilities and undermine them. Children of parents with low self-esteem will have difficulty feeling loved and valued for who they are. For love to be accepted, it must be genuine (Rom. 12:9) and not arise out of self-conceit or envy (Gal. 5:26). It's hard to be yourself when others depend on you to be a certain way to make them feel good. Elaine knew her mom resented her for having a better life than she had. Her mom criticized her for being spoiled and called her a "princess." She ridiculed her ability to play the piano and told her that she had gotten her talent from her but wasn't really as good as she was. The resentment was difficult for Elaine to understand; it was almost as though Elaine had to fail to please her mom.

Parents are also models of either a positive or negative self-image. Perfectionist parents tend to have perfectionist kids. Parents who put themselves down model self-hate and a lack of acceptance. Those who are confident and self-accepting encourage their children to be the same way.

THE IMPACT OF NONACCEPTANCE

We need to be loved, accepted, and acknowledged just because we exist, not because we measure up to someone's standard. When we're not, our self-image suffers. The truth is that other people are flawed humans who may be incapable of loving us and making a right judgment about our worth. Christ accepts us in our sinful state and loved us enough to die for us (Rom. 5:8). God wants us to extend acceptance to each other in the same way Christ accepted us (Rom. 15:7), but people are often unable to do it.

Tina explained her situation this way: "My dad wanted a boy instead of a girl. He rejected everything feminine and tried to push me to play sports. He never told me I looked pretty. He constantly complained about how a boy could have helped him in the family business and would have carried on his name. I tried to be more of what he wanted me to be, but it was never good enough. I realize today that I wasn't flawed; my dad just wasn't capable of loving me. But in my relationships, like my marriage, I'm sensitive to other people not accepting me. I need lots of approval, and it doesn't take much for me to be insecure. I'm always wondering what's wrong with me."

Jack still doubts himself as a result of his divorce. "How can I really be OK if the person I gave my heart and life to decided after living with me that she didn't want me? There has to be something wrong with me, especially since she found another man she says makes her happy in ways that I couldn't." Rejection by a spouse leaves deep wounds in one's self-image that often take a long time to heal.

THE IMPACT OF DYSFUNCTIONAL FAMILIES

Children feel secure when the home environment is predictable and safe and their parents love each other. They feel valued when adults want to spend time with them and give them positive feedback. They feel nurtured when their needs are taken care of. They're able to be themselves when they're free to express their emotions and risk making mistakes by trying new things. They feel loved when they're understood and accepted for who they are with all their strengths and weaknesses.

Dysfunctional families are just the opposite. The parents often have a bad marital relationship that leaves the children feeling insecure. Individuality is not respected. Criticism is rampant, and positive feedback is scarce. Preoccupied parents often neglect children physically or emotionally by not attending to their needs. Emotions and opinions are forbidden, discouraged, or punished. The child is not accepted for who he or she is and is not listened to or understood. Roles are rigid. As a result, children don't feel valued or cared for and conclude that they're unworthy of being loved.

A group of adults who were the products of dysfunctional families described their childhood roles. Jackie discovered parallels between her being a caretaker of her mother and siblings and how she still sees herself as being responsible for everyone in her life. Diana finds herself telling people her opinion about their lives and pointing out their wrongs, just as she did as a child with her alcoholic parents. Ron explained that he always made his family laugh to take the tension away, and he continues to try to gain approval by being witty and funny. Mary realized that she was the one who kept the peace between her parents, and now she finds herself still giving up her needs to keep everyone in her life happy. Jackie's self-image was cast as the responsible one, Diana's as the challenger, Ron's as the clown, and Mary's as the peacemaker.

DAMAGED IMAGES ARE SHAME-BASED

Damaged images result in our carrying a shame-based image of ourselves. Rather than realizing that the *messages* we were given were flawed, we conclude that we are damaged, unlovable, and not good enough. We may feel responsible for other people and their choices. Instead of saying, "They were wrong to hurt me," or "What they said isn't true," we say, "It's my fault they treated me that way," and "What they said must be true." It's common to feel a sense of doom or foreboding about the future, especially when things are going better (Job 3:25). Shame-based people discount or sabotage successes, because they believe that at their core there's nothing good in them. They have damaged self-images resulting from the distorted messages given to them by others.

Shame doesn't feel good. King David said, "Let your face shine on your servant; save me in your unfailing love. Let me not be put to shame, O LORD, for I have cried out to you" (Ps. 31:16-17). God promises to restore you and give you good things (Ps. 103:1-5). Your future isn't one of dread and doom regardless of the damaged images you hold: "'I know the plans I have for you,' declares the LORD, 'plans to prosper you and not to harm you, plans to give you hope and a future'" (Jer. 29:11). Letting go of your damaged image gives you hope for a better tomorrow.

QUESTIONS FOR REFLECTION

1. What are some of the labels others have hung on you that impacted you? How did they shape you?

2. What messages, labels, or words need to be replaced with truth?

3. What are the primary messages significant people in your life have given you? How have those messages impacted your life?

4. Did you receive conflicting messages when you were a child? If so, name them, and describe why they were difficult to deal with.

5. How have the expectations your parents had for you affected your self-image?

6. In what areas do you feel competent versus incompetent? How do you act when you feel confident and when you lack confidence?

7. Have you been abused in any way? How has that abuse affected your self-image?

8. What things did your parents model to you about gender roles? How has that shaped your image of yourself as a woman or a man?

9. Did you feel accepted or rejected by your parents and others at different times of your life? How did that acceptance or rejection define you?

10. Describe your childhood family. What role did you play in that family? Do you still take on that role as an adult?

3

PROJECTED

images

*IT IS GOD'S WILL THAT BY
DOING GOOD YOU SHOULD
SILENCE THE IGNORANT
TALK OF FOOLISH MEN.
LIVE AS FREE MEN.*
—1 PET. 2:15-16

3

PROJECTED

images

IT IS GOD'S WILL THAT BY
DOING GOOD YOU SHOULD
SILENCE THE IGNORANT
TALK OF FOOLISH MEN.
LIVE AS FREE MEN.
—1 PET. 2:15-16

Projected images are those that people project onto us that originate from within them. When you allow the accusations and perceptions of another person to become part of your self-image, you create spiritual and emotional turmoil for yourself and can even place yourself in bondage to others. It is very important to be aware of what others project onto you so you can detach from them and maintain your own image.

BLAME

Emotionally healthy individuals look introspectively at themselves and take responsibility for their own thoughts and behaviors. Persons who lack this important skill project blame onto others.

Blame can be subtle or obvious, occasional or chronic, mild or severe. It can even be as ridiculous as the lazy man who uses the excuse that he can't go to work by saying, "'There is a lion outside!' or 'I will be murdered in the streets!'" (Prov. 22:13). Or it can be as sick and toxic as an abuser who blames his or her destructive actions on the victim by saying, "It's your fault, because if you hadn't done what you did, I wouldn't have had to hurt you."

The purpose of blame is obvious: to avoid responsibility. Prov. 19:3 says, "A man's own folly ruins his life, yet his heart rages against the LORD." Adam and Eve used this defensive response to sin in the Garden of Eden when God confronted them after they ate the forbidden fruit. Even though prior to this incident they hadn't experienced defensiveness or self-consciousness, they instinctively felt uncomfortable admitting the truth about themselves.

Esau and Jacob were brothers. Esau, the firstborn son, was set to inherit his father's blessing and all the perks that went with it. In a weak moment of physical hunger, he fell prey to Jacob's plan to take his birthright for a mere bowl of stew (Gen. 25:29-34). Later, he blamed Jacob for the consequences of his own choice (Gen. 27:36). Esau was unable to see that his actions directly led to his loss, even though Jacob was also responsible for his part in the deception.

Children don't need to be taught to lie and cover up—it comes naturally. When my youngest daughter, Lindsey, was three, she demonstrated this natural tendency to blame her actions on others. She and I had spent an enjoyable afternoon planting spring flowers in our planters. It was fun, and we talked about how pretty they were. She was especially proud of herself, as she had planted many of the flowers on her own. The next afternoon I was shocked to find all the flowers dug up. When I asked Lindsey about it, she denied doing it and blamed it on Foxie, our fox terrier. That might have been a plausible possibility, except for one problem: Foxie had died three months earlier. Apparently, Lindsey had much to learn about shifting blame creatively and believably.

FEELINGS

Persons often blame others for their own feelings. We all say things like "He made me mad." "She hurt me." "She makes me unhappy." "He makes me feel bad about myself." These kinds of comments imply that we have no choice in how we feel and that others have control over us. In reality, we have control—they don't. Feelings can be strong and arise quickly, so it's easy to think the other person is responsible, but that isn't true.

"A wicked man puts up a bold front, but an upright man gives thought to his ways" (Prov. 21:29). It's essential that we analyze our feelings honestly so we won't foolishly blame others for our feelings.

Your responses are usually affected by your temperament, past experiences, state of mind and body, and perceptions. Your feelings are related to what you think about a situation and how you interpret what's happening. Someone else in the same situation might react differently, and you might, too, on another day.

Anytime someone is hurt or angry, part of the offense lies in the way he or she interprets what was done. Anger stems from the belief that an injustice was done. Hurt stems from the belief that the person intended harm.

What we think directly affects our feelings. Here's an example: A man driving down the road is cut off by a car and slams on his brakes. He thinks, *How dare he do that? What a jerk!* He feels anger and irritation. I wonder how he might have felt if instead his thoughts were *That guy must have a lot on his mind not to notice me.* He might have felt compassion, patience, and tolerance.

What makes the difference in a wife's feelings about her husband coming home from work late? If she thinks, *He's working so hard—poor guy,* she'll feel tolerant and accepting. But if she thinks, *He's so inconsiderate,* she'll be angry. Your feelings are your choice and your responsibility regardless of what the person does. Other people's feelings are theirs, and you're not responsible for them.

When someone accuses you of making him or her feel a certain way, you may be tempted to feel responsible—but you are not responsible. That's not always easy to remember when people choose to blame you for their moods, anger, and distress. The truth is that their emotions and responses have everything to do with what they think, what's going on with their own lives, how they interpret what's going on, and what they feel as a result. Even if you did something wrong, the other person's reaction is his or her responsibility and choice. Each of us will give an account for his or her own actions, not the actions of others (Matt. 12:36).

There are always options. People can be angry or understanding, punitive or forgiving, sarcastic or kind, passive or assertive. Jeanette's husband goes through periods in his work when an already taxing and stressful job spirals into an impossibly demanding schedule. He predictably becomes critical and unhappy with her during those times. Jeanette can choose to accept his blame and feel badly about herself, or she can listen to his specific concerns but not necessarily take them on as fact. She can choose to realize that some of his unhappiness is a result of his being overstressed and overtired. Jeanette is still responsible for how she reacts to him, though. She can get angry in turn or let him work through his own emotions. It would be nice if he recognized that his feelings are related to what's going on with him at the time, but he doesn't always do that. So Jeanette can protect herself by recognizing the variables for what they are rather than taking on all his projections.

UNTRUE ACCUSATIONS

"You're a mean and selfish person—you don't care about your family," Bob's mother says to him after he tells her he can't come home that weekend because he's busy with his wife and kids. Bob thinks, *I should figure out how to see my parents more—I'm an ungrateful son.*

Carol's husband tells her for the thousandth time, "You aren't a good wife. You don't treat me the way a man needs to be treated. You shouldn't argue with me and tell me what to do!" Carol was merely stating her opinion, and her husband doesn't like her to tell him what she thinks. *I'm nagging,* she says to herself. *I shouldn't have said anything.*

Jen's sister says, "You're jealous of me and want me to fail so I won't do better than you." Jen feels confused, because she knows she doesn't want her sister to fail, but she concludes that she must be jealous since her sister believes she is.

People accuse us of many things. Bob, Carol, and Jen have all been accused by people close to them of having negative motives, characteristics, and actions. The important thing to note is that these accusations may not be true. In all these examples, the people making the accusations hold specific beliefs, expectations, and interpretations that may have more to do with themselves than the persons they're accusing. When others project accusations onto you, analyze them before you take them on as part of your self-image. Bob, Carol, and Jen weren't able to choose their own perceptions over the other person's, so they accepted the projected accusations as part of their own self-image.

Bob's mother is unreasonable and very demanding of Bob's time. She's unwilling to accept that he has responsibilities to his wife and children. If Bob feels badly about himself every time his mother is unhappy with him, he is accepting a wrong image of himself.

Carol's husband accuses her of being a nag when she shares her thoughts with him. The truth is, he believes he has the right as a man to do whatever he wants without Carol's telling him her opinion. His inaccurate view of submission is unreasonable. If Carol accepts his conclusion that she's a bad wife, her image of herself will be distorted, because it's based on her husband's inaccurate beliefs about marriage and about her.

Jen rightfully checked her motives to see if she was jealous, but she still chose her sister's perception over her own, even though she disagreed.

Someone may say, "You were making fun of me" or "You ignored me" or "You wanted me to fail." Only you know your motives; others can only guess. Because someone else feels ridiculed, put down, or ignored doesn't mean you did it. It could be his or her feelings of rejection or sensitivity. Others may perceive something as purposeful, but you might have been innocently minding your own business, doing what you thought you needed to do, or were just unaware of how the person was affected by your actions. When someone projects a motive onto you, analyze it yourself to see if it was true, and then admit only what's true for you. You don't have to accept someone else's perception of your behavior as more valid than your own.

Persons often project the parts of themselves that they refuse to accept onto others and often criticize the characteristics in others that they most dislike in themselves. Prov. 26:24 says, "A malicious man disguises himself with his lips, but in his heart he harbors deceit." Deceptive people may project their dishonesty onto you by accusing you of being untruthful, manipulative, and deceitful. Knowing they aren't trustworthy leads them to be suspicious of others. Unfaithful partners often accuse their spouses of having affairs. Selfish people often accuse others of being selfish even when they're simply stating opinions or taking care of themselves in healthful ways. Controlling people accuse others of trying to control them. Jealous people see others as competitive.

People may accuse you of things for many reasons. They may use guilt or manipulation to get what they want, avoid responsibility, or take control. They could be sincere but misguided due to their unreasonable demands, expectations, and beliefs. They could be projecting their insecurities from past relationships onto you. They may be dysfunctional, addicted, emotionally ill, abusive, self-centered, immature, or malicious. Or they may simply have different perspectives, values, and standards than you.

Jesus was misunderstood and falsely accused by the religious teachers of His day (Luke 6:7). They even accused Him of having an evil spirit (Mark 3:22, 30). There are those who will accuse you of doing evil when you're actually doing good. It's better to endure the untrue accusations and do what's right than to do what's wrong to avoid the accusations and displeasure of those who are unhappy with your choices (1 Pet. 3:14-17).

When someone accuses you, consider whether it could be the person's own issues projected onto you. If you accept false accusations as fact, you'll believe things about yourself that are inaccurate and have a faulty self-image as a result. Remember—just because someone says it doesn't make it so.

UNRESOLVED WOUNDS

No one goes through life without wounds, and "Each heart knows its own bitterness" (Prov. 14:10). We didn't have perfect parents, nor do we live in a perfect world, nor are *we* perfect. Each of us has times when we're criticized, treated unfairly, rejected, abandoned, hurt, or misunderstood.

We carry the wounds from our pasts in our psyches and react emotionally to current events based on our past experiences. When you interact with another, you're dealing with someone who is who he or she is in the moment because of all his or her life experiences. That person brings along his or her hurts, wounds, sensitivities, memories, and needs into the present situation. His or her past is a time bomb waiting to go off when something familiar triggers a negative memory and the accompanying emotions.

Here are some typical overreactions that originate more from past emotions and experiences than the current situation:

- A husband is talking to a woman after church. His wife is convinced that he's going to have an affair. She threatens to divorce him unless he promises never to speak to the woman again. Her husband isn't unfaithful, but her prior marriage ended because her husband had an affair, and she's insecure.

- A woman tells her roommate she's moving out. The roommate responds that she never wants to see the woman again and accuses her of abandonment. Her father abandoned her when she was three years old.

- An adult daughter is late coming home one night, and her mother panics, thinking she's been in a car wreck. When the daughter arrives home, her mother accuses her of being selfish and insensitive. The mother's sister was killed in a car accident when she was 13 years old.

- A husband comments that he doesn't really like the dinner his wife cooked, and she reacts with a tirade of accusations: "You don't appreciate me or love me. Nothing I do pleases you. I'm never cooking for you again." Her father was extremely critical and rejecting.

These are examples of overreaction; the person responded in a way that the present circumstances didn't warrant. Something done consciously or unconsciously reminded the person of something or someone in the past, and the emotion from that circumstance was triggered by the brain, bringing the old feelings into the present. The emotions and perceptions of the past were then transferred onto the other person.

The reaction is most likely related to the past when it has the following characteristics:

- It is an overreaction to the current circumstances.
- The issue is a hot button that surfaces repeatedly.
- The issue is difficult to resolve.
- The person is overly defensive and sensitive.
- Physical symptoms accompany the response: panic, nausea, instant rage, numbness, a tight throat, or a gut feeling.

For example, you comment on a job your spouse did, indicating that it was OK but could be better. Your spouse, who was criticized relentlessly by his or her father, is sensitive to criticism. Your criticism may be constructive and accurate. But your spouse, who is used to feeling demeaned by harsh criticism, responds as if you're attacking him or her. You may get a reaction like "Don't put me down. I don't do anything right for you—you're just hard to please." This is a case of bringing unresolved issues of the past into the present.

This also happens with people who are overly sensitive to how they are treated. Someone who always feels slighted or overlooked may accuse you of abandonment, rudeness, or self-centeredness because he or she needs an excessive amount of reassurance, attention, and approval. Or someone spoken to disrespectfully or abusively in the past may feel put down by the slightest suggestion of strength or assertiveness in you and be overly sensitive to your tone of voice and accuse you of being rude when you're speaking assertively or naturally. If you take on these beliefs about yourself, you'll take on an incorrect self-image.

POWER AND AUTHORITY

An authority figure is someone who has power over you emotionally, spiritually, mentally, physically, or materially. The power can be perceived or actual. Perceived power is when you *feel* intimidated by the person because he or she knows more than you, or you *feel* he or she is better than you, but the person doesn't have the power to impose direct consequences. Persons who could impose consequences hold *actual* power. Authority figures include parents, spouse, boss, church leaders, people in power, policemen, the government, leaders of organizations, people who are considered to be authorities in certain fields, and anyone else you feel has an influential hold on you because of his or her position or ability to affect your life.

God established authority to maintain order and punish wrongdoers. We're supposed to submit to and respect authority. We can be free from the fear of authority, according to Rom. 13:1-7, by doing what is right, which is usually to obey authority. But we also know from Peter's encounter with the leaders of his day that there are times we must refuse to obey authority and instead obey God and follow our consciences. When the apostles were told not to preach about Jesus after being released from jail, they openly defied the order, stating, "We must obey God rather than men!" (Acts 5:29). We also know from history that power is frequently abused by sinful people, so we must be on guard and be as shrewd as snakes (Matt. 10:16-17).

When an authority figure is wrong, it's necessary to stand up to him or her and follow your conscience instead. This can be difficult if you've been abused or mistreated by a prior authority figure, because you'll be more vulnerable to believing anything an authority figure tells you and less able to independently determine what's right and wrong.

MANIPULATION AND GUILT

Some people will project guilt onto you in order to manipulate you into doing what they want through accusations, demands, threats, subtle suggestions, emotional withdrawal, disapproval, or by feigning helplessness.

People who are victims, martyrs, dependent, and irresponsible have something in common: They don't want to be responsible for themselves. Instead, they want you to feel responsible and be responsible for them, so they hand it off to you by projecting guilt.

Victims, like martyrs, choose to believe they have no other choices and refuse to exercise their power to make changes. Both want you to feel sorry for them and will continually try to hook you into feeling pity and doing things for them. Irresponsible people refuse to exercise self-control and self-discipline. Dependent people are needy and don't see themselves as capable of taking care of themselves. Both will project their needs onto you. Truthfully, each person is responsible for taking care of himself or herself (1 Thess. 4:11-12).

If you find yourself continually doing things for another but feeling angry or resentful about it, and you feel guilty for saying no or struggle with feelings of obligation, you may be dealing with someone who is using guilt to manipulate you into doing things he or she should be doing for himself or herself. When that person projects the responsibility onto you, and you take it on, you lose some of your objective ability to make a healthful choice and instead do it because you feel you have to, not because you want to.

For example: Your mother suggests that she doesn't need

your help with your sick father because, after all, she has handled him for years without help. You know she refuses to use her money to get help, even though she could, and that she always makes comments like these no matter how much you do. More times than not, you inconvenience your own family to go help her, even though you resent it. The guilt she projects on you results in your feeling badly about yourself, but you also feel badly that you resent her. Now you've become a martyr and a victim too! When she projects her feelings of self-pity, dependency, and martyrdom onto you, recognize them as inaccurate. She has choices, and so do you. The only way to feel good about what you do is to independently, without succumbing to projected guilt and manipulation, choose to do what's right for you. Then you do it because you *want* to (2 Cor. 9:7). Your yes and no will be sincere (Matt. 5:37).

CRITICISM

Critical people judge others. The implication when you're criticized is that you're wrong, but you might not be. Criticism says more about the person doing the criticizing than you, because the critical person is expressing his or her standards, values, opinions, expectations, and weaknesses.

Cammy found herself criticizing the way other women dressed; she was extremely critical of her own looks and spent lots of time and money on her appearance.

Gene pushed himself relentlessly to achieve, never allowing himself to relax and enjoy life; he found himself extremely critical of lazy and unproductive people and judged anyone who didn't work as hard as he did.

Hannah criticized judgmental people; but she was the most judgmental of all.

Debra gossiped about people who couldn't keep anything to themselves, even though she couldn't either.

The things a person criticizes others for are often the things in which that very person continually falls short. While it may be hard to believe when you're the object of criticism, people like that are usually hardest on themselves.

ANGER

Anger easily projects onto you because it's an intense emotion, and it's contagious because it feels threatening and provokes a defensive response. Proverbs 15:1 says, "A harsh word stirs up anger." Being around an angry person can result in your becoming angrier yourself (Prov. 22:24-25).

Angry persons often want others to be angry along with them. An angry husband says to his wife, "You're mad at me again." She denies it, because she knows she's not mad, but as he continues to interact angrily with her and accuse her of being angry, she finally realizes, "I wasn't angry to start with, but I am now." Angry people tend to blame their anger on others to get them to react. This husband can walk away feeling justified because he was right—she's angry, and why wouldn't he be angry with her in return? Then, if he wants to use her anger as an excuse to withdraw, engage in an addiction, or mistreat her, he feels justified in doing so.

Ray pushed Celene's buttons until she blew up at him and told him he was a jerk. Then he called her a nag and said, "Who wouldn't need to drink if they lived with you?" He headed out with the guys to drink, feeling justified.

It's also common to feel responsible for another person's anger. The result is low self-image that reminds you that you did something wrong—again. The truth is—people are angry because they're angry; it isn't necessarily your fault.

Kyle was often mad about something and often took it out on his family. His wife always tried to figure out what she did wrong and tried to do better so he wouldn't blow. She didn't understand that his anger originated within him and that she was just a convenient target. No matter what she did, she wouldn't be able to please him and keep him from being angry.

Passive-aggressive anger projects onto you, even though the person denies he or she is angry. As the recipient, you'll feel the anger and hostility and become angry in return. Proverbs 15:4 says, "A deceitful tongue crushes the spirit." Underlying passive-aggressiveness is the fear of dependency, the fear of being controlled, and the fear of being hurt. As a result, passive-aggressive people see you as a threat and the aggressor, so they won't admit to being wrong or show remorse. They're unwilling to openly admit they're angry, so instead, they passively resist and thwart your efforts while pretending to cooperate.

Passive-aggressive persons may show up late, be uncooperative, forget to do what you ask them to do, or purposefully do it wrong, lie, make excuses, or withdraw. They're sensitive to criticism and will find a way to make your legitimate complaints about them your fault. They become infuriated when confronted with anything they did wrong and will accuse you of being mean and aggressive. Their behavior is confusing and infuriating to you, and by the time it gets to this point, you may actually be the one who is out of control, crazy, and angry. And there you are, exactly where they want you to be. They have successively projected their anger onto you and proven that you're the aggressor they imagined you to be.

Charlie never cooperated with Tricia's requests. He would drag his feet, forget to do what she asked, and ignore her when she talked. She found herself fuming and finally screaming at him. He acted innocent and wounded, not understanding why she was so "nuts." Tricia couldn't explain it, but she felt as if Charlie did it purposefully, and it was infuriating to her that he wouldn't admit it.

SUPERIORITY

Arrogant and proud people often have very low self-esteem. Yet because of their deep feelings of inferiority, they portray the opposite. Their inferiority is often projected onto others so that they can maintain the illusion of superiority.

When someone acts as if he or she is better than you, it triggers the weaknesses in your self-image. If you feel inferior, it's probably because you perceive the other person as being better than you. Obviously, if someone arrogantly flaunts an income that's less than yours, you won't feel inferior. But if someone who's good at sports brags about his or her sports achievement, and you perceive yourself as not being good in sports and wish you were, you're likely to feel badly about yourself as you interact with that person. If you act superior, you're reacting defensively to them to protect yourself from feeling inferior.

Narcissists are self-centered people who have little room for others. Everything is about them; nothing is about you. They need to be the center of attention and treated as if they're special. If you've been parented by or married to a narcissist, you may have difficulty knowing who you are as a person and believing that your needs are important. When someone important to you projects on-to you the belief that you don't matter, you'll struggle with whether or not you do. Love can't exist in a relationship where selfishness and self-seeking is the center of the relationship (1 Cor. 13:5).

Gavin ignored Sabrina's needs and continually accused her of being selfish. He talked constantly about himself and was very sensitive to not being treated "special" as he deserved, yet he treated her as if she didn't matter at all. It was a struggle for Sabrina to get any of her needs met in their marriage. Gavin was indifferent to her tears and pleas and completely oblivious to the pain she experienced. She eventually gave up and decided she didn't really matter and did whatever he wanted just to keep the peace.

ALL BAD OR ALL GOOD

Some persons have difficulty putting the good and bad to-gether and will instead split themselves and others into "all good" or "all bad." When they're doing well, they see themselves as good. But when they're doing poorly, they see themselves as bad. Some-times seeing good in you will result in their feeling bad about them-selves—which feels intolerable. So they project the "badness" onto you. These people tend to be defensive and have difficulty hearing criticism or addressing any of their own faults. They have trouble looking within introspectively, because when they see anything bad in themselves, they go directly to seeing themselves as all bad.

Typical comments to a criticism of "You didn't put the kids to bed on time" would be "I'm not a bad father. You're saying I'm a bad father." In reality, the wife didn't say anything about his ability as a father, only that he didn't put the kids to bed on time. A hus-band could say, "Honey, why is the house so messy?" and she would respond with "I never please you. I'm a failure as a wife." The difficulty when interacting with someone who sees people as either all good or all bad is that you can never resolve issues. You find yourself having circular conversations about who is at fault, who is blaming who, who is the bad guy and good guy, and taking on their projections. It goes nowhere.

In reality, none of us—not even the worst criminal—is all bad. Everyone has some redeeming qualities. Conversely, none of us—except Christ—is all good. When someone tries to make you all bad, understand you aren't. If you begin to judge yourself as all good or all bad, try to stop and integrate your two parts: the good and the bad, with strengths and weaknesses. This way you won't accept a flawed self-image with inaccurate perceptions.

REJECTING PROJECTED IMAGES

Projected images come in a variety of forms that can be subtle or obvious. Because they conflict with your own images, they create emotional turmoil, stress, and confusion. If you allow the images to be projected onto you, you lose your own real self-image. When someone is projecting an image onto you, it's important to recognize it and detach from it before you accept it as your own.

Detachment is about stepping back from the situation and observing it as if you were an outsider. You let go of feeling responsible for the other person's feelings, moods, problems, perceptions, and choices. Instead, you focus on yourself—*your* feelings, moods, problems, perceptions, and choices. You trust what you feel.

If you see that someone is angry, you allow the person to own his or her anger and refuse to take responsibility for it. Don't assume you caused it or that it's your job to defuse it. Instead, step back and focus on yourself, paying attention to your feelings. Examine your attitude when dealing with the person.

If someone is accusing you, blaming you for his or her feelings or choices or criticizing you, give yourself time to process what was said, and then decide whether or not it's true. Even if you feel you contributed to the situation and did something wrong, you're still not responsible for the other person's feeling, reaction, or perception about it.

If someone is trying to hook you into taking care of him or her by helplessness, complaints, hints, manipulation, or guilt, step back and decide whether you want to do something for him or her rather than taking on the guilt and feeling compelled to do what you don't want to do.

If someone is overreacting to something you did, try to understand how his or her wounds affect these perceptions of you and the situation, offer empathy and understanding, and then reject the projection of that perception onto you.

If a person is projecting his or her superiority onto you, be aware of it, and don't play the "I'm better [worse] than you" game. Instead, see the person as he or she really is: insecure. Be willing to question authority figures and stand up for what's right if what they are saying or doing is wrong.

If someone tries to project an all-bad or all-good image onto you, reject it. Don't discuss the relationship from that polarized view. Instead, stick to the details of what happened. If the conversation continually gets brought back to that circular argument, step out of the argument by removing yourself.

At times, detachment will be physical and other times emotional or mental. Physical detachment means you leave the room to get actual distance between yourself and the other person. This is necessary when emotions run high and the situation requires a time-out so you won't react and can also be a means of protecting yourself if the other person is a threat to you. It's also a good idea when the presence of the other person and the situation is causing you emotional confusion and you need time to sort out your feelings and thoughts. In this situation, having a trusted third party—a mentor, friend, or counselor—to talk to is often helpful.

When the Israelites traveled in the wilderness, they were restless, unhappy, angry, blaming, and irresponsible victims. They continually grumbled among themselves and projected their problems, feelings, and accusations onto Moses and Aaron. Whether it was fear, fatigue, hunger, or thirst, it was Moses' fault for bringing them out of Egypt in the first place. Moses could have believed their problems were his fault and that he was a failure, but he didn't. Instead, he told them where their complaining was really directed: "You are not grumbling against us, but against the LORD" (Exod. 16:8). But time and time again, the people turned on Moses and Aaron when things got difficult. Instead of trusting God, they blamed Moses and Aaron for their discomfort, fear, and discontent.

When others project their "stuff" onto you, it doesn't mean you've done something wrong. You don't have to adjust your self-image to fit the junk that gets thrown at you; if you do, you'll suffer. Moses did pretty well with not allowing the Israelites to project their anger and discontent onto him. But one day it was too much for even him (Num. 20:1-13). When the people ran out of water again, they began to murmur against Moses and Aaron, arguing, complaining, blaming, and feeling sorry for themselves. Moses and Aaron went to the Lord, as they usually did, and God faithfully came through with another miraculous provision for His weak and faithless people. He told Moses to speak to the rock, and water would gush out. Moses went, intending to be obedient to God, but then it got to be too much for him. He took the Israelites' complaints to heart and got defensive. He angrily said, "'Listen, you rebels, must we bring you water out of this rock?' Then Moses raised his arm and struck the rock twice with his staff. Water gushed out, and the community and their livestock drank. But the LORD said to Moses and Aaron, 'Because you did not trust in me enough to honor me as holy in the sight of the Israelites, you will not bring this community into the land I give them'" (Num. 20:10-12).

Moses messed up. He reacted to their emotional discontent as if it were personal. He took on their anger as his own so that instead of speaking to the rock as God directed, he hit it with his staff. Moses and Aaron trusted God; they weren't in a state of panic, doubt, or discontent, but they got that way by taking on the projected feelings of others.

This is what you do when you allow others to project their feelings and inadequacies onto you: You pick it up and make it your own and then suffer because of it. It's better to allow others to be responsible for where they are, to pay attention to what you feel and think separately from them, and to refuse to allow them to project their "stuff" onto you. Instead, decide what you want to do and be. Then you'll be rejecting their projected images.

QUESTIONS FOR REFLECTION

1. When have you been blamed by others for their choices and feelings? How does accepting that blame affect your self-image?

2. Think of times people have made untrue accusations about you. Was it difficult to hold to your own perceptions in spite of what they thought about you? How did it affect your self-image when you accepted their accusations?

3. Think of situations when you and your loved ones over-reacted. How do these hot-button situations affect your self-image?

4. How does dealing with an authority figure affect you? Do you feel intimidated and inferior, or can you stand up for your beliefs?

5. Think of situations in which people try to manipulate you into taking care of them or taking over their responsibilities by projecting guilt onto you. How do you react? How does it affect your self-image?

6. How do you respond inwardly and outwardly to criticism? Can you separate someone else's opinion about you from your opinion of yourself?

7. How does anger affect you? Do you become angry and defensive, take responsibility for the person's anger, or shut down?

8. What is your experience with narcissistic, self-centered, and arrogant people? How do you feel about yourself when someone ignores you and acts as if you're irrelevant and inferior or acts superior to you?

9. Describe your experiences with people who see you as all bad or all good. Are they able to successfully project their perception onto you?

10. If detachment means you separate yourself physically, emotionally, and mentally from other people's projections, are you able to detach? How does that protect your self-image?

4

REFLECTED

images

SEE TO IT THAT NO ONE TAKES YOU CAPTIVE THROUGH HOLLOW AND DECEPTIVE PHILOSOPHY, WHICH DEPENDS ON HUMAN TRADITION AND THE BASIC PRINCIPLES OF THIS WORLD RATHER THAN ON CHRIST.

—COL. 2:8

4

REFLECTED images

SEE TO IT THAT NO ONE TAKES YOU
CAPTIVE THROUGH HOLLOW AND
DECEPTIVE PHILOSOPHY, WHICH
DEPENDS ON HUMAN TRADITION
AND THE BASIC PRINCIPLES OF THIS
WORLD RATHER THAN ON CHRIST.
—COL. 2:8

Reflected images are the images we use to measure our self-worth. We're bombarded with images of the perfect body, marriage, home, career, and life. The values emphasized are often material and superficial. Cultural stereotypes define what is good, bad, and valued. The Church presents an image of the ideal Christian, wife, husband, and parent, inadvertently inflicting condemnation and guilt on those who fall short of this modern-day legalism much as the Pharisees promoted a hypocritical and superficial religiosity. We all hold an image in our minds of our ideal selves, and we feel badly when we fall short. Perfectionism, an impossible standard, is a mirror that reminds us of our shortcomings. When you measure yourself against these standards or compare yourself to others, you lose.

IDEAL BEAUTY

Our society is obsessed with outward beauty. Think of shows like *Extreme Makeover* and the billions of dollars spent on plastic surgery each year in the United States. I asked a plastic surgeon at what age people stop focusing on how they look, and he said, "Never. I do surgery on people in their 80s all the time." I was amazed when I heard about a mom who told her daughter to consider becoming a candidate for *Extreme Makeover*. My heart goes out to that girl. Her mother has confirmed that not only is she not beautiful, she is so flawed that only a surgical makeover will solve her problems.

As young as age five or six, kids become aware that their peers value certain characteristics and that if they don't have them, they're inferior. Even nine-year-olds worry about their weight.

God made us to appreciate beauty. Yet He didn't make everyone beautiful—by our standards. I was recently at a water park with my daughter and her friends. Many of the kids at the park were preteens and teens, all in bathing suits. I can tell you that in that group of more than a thousand teens, I saw only a few who would qualify as ideal. Where does that leave most of us if we measure our worth by outward appearance? It leaves us feeling inferior, un-accepted, and flawed. No wonder anorexia, bulimia, depression, and self-mutilation are rampant among our teens.

Is your idea of perfection the images you see on the maga-zine covers at the grocery store checkout? If you're like most peo-ple, you've measured yourself and probably your spouse against these images. For women, the perfect body is tall, thin, large-breasted, and physically fit. For men, the perfect body is tall with a masculine build and lots of hair. Very few of us reflect that perfect image. And even the people who do—like the supermodels—re-port that they wrestle with deep insecurities.

Sheila Walsh, a Christian singer, author, and Women of Faith speaker, says that her first album shoot was devastating. All she could see and hear were people looking at her and saying, "Fix this mark," "Change those clothes," "Make this less obvious." After hours of make-up and wardrobe changes and photographers trying to get the perfect angle, she walked away convinced she was hopelessly flawed.

Culturally defined standards of beauty vary. In the past, skinny wasn't considered beautiful. Eating disorders and the preoccupa-tion with weight and body shape increase in societies undergoing Westernization. Normal weight is different for every person, yet as many as seven out of ten women are on a diet at any given time.

Assessing self-worth from outward appearance is a guaran-teed lose-lose deal. Even if you have "it" at some point, as you grow old you'll lose it. If I could have a dollar for every second I've wasted on worrying about how I look, I would be rich. I imagine you would too. The futile pursuit of beauty, love, and approval through external appearance often causes us to make wrong choices: pornography, flirtatiousness, promiscuousness, immodest dress, and materialism.

Wanting to live forever and look young doing it is not new. Ponce de Leon traveled the world looking for the fountain of youth. Our bodies grow old, but our spirits and the will to live do not. God has placed eternity in our hearts; we want to live forever. My daughter once said, "Gramma isn't old, because she doesn't act old." My mom said, "I feel like myself but in an old body." Both are simple statements yet profound: She is *herself*. The body is a deteriorating shell, but the soul isn't. She will live forever in a regenerated body (1 Cor. 15:53-54).

Men care about their looks, but overall they care less than women. Instead, a man tends to measure his worth based on achievements, material possessions, money, and having a nice-looking woman at his side. Feeding one's self-image from those external things is problematic. Focusing on the need for a beautiful woman can get a man sidetracked, as it did for David with Bathsheba. David's temporal focus on his fleshly desire for a beautiful woman led to adultery, murder, the death of his sons, conspiracy, and disgrace (2 Sam. 11—12). Adjusting your values to find continual satisfaction with your spouse for your whole life is the better choice (Eccles. 9:9; Prov. 5:19). As Solomon, David and Bathsheba's son, discovered, if one pursues self-worth and meaning through the accumulation of material possessions, money, and achievements, life is empty and meaningless (Eccles. 2:1-11).

REAL BEAUTY

What is true beauty? As individuals and as a society, how do we convince ourselves that inner beauty matters more than outer beauty? We're handicapped by our sight. God reminds us to look on the inside rather than the outside to judge a person's heart (1 Sam. 16:7), but we must become blind to outward appearances to do that.

Without mirrors and photographs, we wouldn't know how we look. That is an intriguing proposition. I believe it would change my perception of myself. What about you?

If you're a woman, rather than comparing yourself to the air-brushed magazine models or celebrities, compare yourself to the Prov. 31 woman whose description says nothing about her physical beauty. Instead, she's a faithful wife, productive, wise, strong, an effective manager of her home and work, a good mother, a volunteer, respectable, full of integrity, knowledgeable, and able to face the future with confidence. This sums it up: "Charm is deceptive, and beauty is fleeting; but a woman who fears the LORD is to be praised" (Prov. 31:30). Those are all things you can work toward, not things you're born with and lose, such as physical beauty.

Men, instead of comparing yourself to other men based on your wife's looks, the size of your paycheck, and your measure of material success, compare yourself to the description of a man worthy of being a church elder, found in 1 Tim. 3:2-4 and Titus 1:6-9. This man is faithful to his wife, self-controlled, a good father and manager of his home, respectable, gentle, not obsessed with money, not addicted to alcohol or other things, not argumentative, hospitable, honest, disciplined, and knowledgeable about God. Those are all character traits that can be learned; none are traits you are born with. All of us can become inwardly beautiful and successful in God's economy.

The pursuit of physical beauty will leave you feeling inadequate and empty. So what's the solution? The Serenity Prayer by Reinhold Niebuhr says to ask God to give you the serenity to accept the things you cannot change, the courage to change the things you can, and the wisdom to know the difference. Thank God that you're fearfully and uniquely made (Ps. 139:14), accept yourself for who you are, and devote yourself to becoming more Christlike in every area of your life.

You can change your clothes, makeup, hairstyle, and sometimes your weight. There's nothing wrong with looking your best and doing what you can to be attractive, as long as it's modest, appropriate, balanced, and you realize that your true beauty doesn't come from your outward appearance but rather the inward beauty of "a gentle and quiet spirit" (1 Pet. 3:3-4). You can't change your height, body build, or age.

You can change all kinds of things on the inside: your spirit, priorities, personal characteristics, choices, attitudes, the manner in which you treat others, and your values.

THE COMPARISON TRAP

If you don't compare yourself to the reflected images around you, you won't fall short. That's worth saying again in a slightly different way so it sinks in: *Comparison* is the problem. *Not comparing yourself to others* is the solution.

Comparison has two outcomes: You're either better than the other person or worse than the other person. You'll feel either superior or inferior. If you compare yourself to a supermodel, you'll fall short; if you compare yourself to the least attractive person at the grocery store, you'll feel better. Feeling neither better nor worse than others is a truthful assessment: "If anyone thinks he is something when he is nothing, he deceives himself. Each one should test his own actions. Then he can take pride in himself, without comparing himself to somebody else" (Gal. 6:3-4).

One woman grasped that idea. After some deep thought, she said, "I get it. I compare myself to myself. Then, if I improve, I can feel better; if I slip back, I can be motivated to try to do better again. It feels as though I can finally win! I've always compared myself to people who seem so much better than me that I felt discouraged and gave up."

Comparison results in pride, self-pity, jealousy, and competitiveness. God has told us not to covet what our neighbor has (Exod. 20:17). All these things are part of our old sin nature (Gal. 5:19-21). The result is discord and strife in our relationships. Have you ever experienced the inability to have a good relationship with someone because your envy got in the way or because your feelings of superiority made it difficult for you to treat the other person as an equal? I have.

Another problem with comparisons is that they aren't fair. When you compare your insides with my outsides, you see the put-together external I *want* you to see. Just like the airbrushed magazine photos of people who have undergone hours of professional makeup and dress from a personal stylist, you don't see the real deal. It's not a fair comparison, because you know all your own internal and external flaws. You don't stand a chance of measuring up to the external facade of someone else who's showing only what he or she wants you to see.

I've made comparisons many times on Sunday mornings at

church. When I'm dissatisfied with my husband and marriage, I find myself looking around and seeing all the "happy" couples at church. I idealize them to be perfect, and my dissatisfaction with my husband grows. I know all of them have some problems, and many of their marriages are far more troubled than mine. Many of these couples may have fought all the way to church. But on the outside they look good to me. I probably look good to them. When I'm unhappy with myself for something like losing my temper with my kids, I look around and see all the other "nice" mothers and feel badly about myself, imagining that they never do what I did. When you compare the real you to the outside facade of others, you're cheating yourself.

The Pharisees made this mistake by thinking that their external righteous deeds would get them approved by God. They ignored what was in their hearts. Jesus set them straight: He told them to clean the inside first, and then the outside would be automatically clean (Matt. 23:25-26). If you compare your inside to others' outsides, you can easily be fooled, because the outside is much easier to clean up superficially than is the heart.

THE IDEAL CHRISTIAN

There are reflected images at church too. "Ideal Christians" love God with all their hearts, read the Bible and pray every day for an hour, raise their children in the Lord, tithe more than 10 percent, help the poor, show up at church to volunteer regularly, attend church and Bible study faithfully, witness to everyone they meet, are never depressed or discouraged, trust God completely, and are never afraid.

Comparing yourself to the ideal may discourage you and bring condemnation (Luke 11:46). You may feel guilty when you don't read your Bible, pray, and witness, and you'll feel that God is unhappy with you. That guilt pulls you farther away from Him, not closer. If you believe you shouldn't be fearful, discouraged, and depressed, but always happy, joyful, and trusting no matter what, you won't be able to be honest about your struggles and weaknesses and won't turn to God and others for support. King David experienced all those emotions. He, like us, was a work in progress. He faced times of anger, depression, discouragement, despair, despondency, fear, and jealousy. Yet throughout his emotional roller-coaster ride, he continued to trust God, and eventually his despair turned to joy (Ps. 31). But for a while he was in the pits.

Joy isn't the same as happiness. Happiness is transitory; joy is deep trust and peace, knowing that no matter what happens, God is on your side, and you have everything you need from Him (Phil. 4:19). You can be in deep pain and still have joy (Phil. 4:4-7).

Betty didn't understand this, so she didn't allow herself to admit she was unhappy or discouraged, because she always "rejoiced in the Lord." She grit her teeth and smiled no matter what she felt inside, even looking around at others with a judgmental attitude, thinking, *Why aren't they happy like me?* But she also felt very lonely and couldn't understand why no one at church seemed to care about her. Betty's inability to be honest about her emotions kept her isolated from others.

The ideal Christian marriage doesn't exist. If a wife measures her husband against the spiritual ideal, she'll be unhappy with him. Most men don't fit the image of the perfect spiritual leader put forth in the Church. Some don't have the knowledge, spiritual maturity, or the personality to lead their families spiritually but are nevertheless good providers, husbands, and fathers, and need to be acknowledged as such. A wife's discontent with her husband will affect their relationship, and he won't feel respected or appreciated, both of which are deep needs in the heart of a man. If a husband equates a godly wife with being quiet, submissive, and supportive of everything he does, without ever complaining or voicing an opinion, he won't encourage her to be his partner and will be unable to hear her needs, and she won't feel loved.

Comparing your life to an ideal means you lose. The same goes for materialism. We all envision ourselves with the American dream: obedient children, a large home, nice cars, family vacations, and retirement money in the bank. If you assume that God's blessing equals material success, you'll be even more disillusioned if you fall short. The key is to learn to be content with what you have right now whether it's a lot or a little or more or less than what you've had in the past or would like to have (Phil. 4:11-13). The only way to do that is to *not* compare yourself to others or an ideal.

Patty was relieved. "I do have those ideals in my head! I can't believe how much guilt I carry for not measuring up to all of them. It feels good to accept myself and my husband as we are. We're not perfect, but we're still together and struggling to do better. I've been mad at him for not leading family devotions, but when I really think about it, he's a quiet guy, and that isn't his style. He's good about doing things with the kids, though, and he works hard to send them to Christian school."

Like Patty, I was discontented with my husband's "spiritual leadership" style. He didn't lead family devotions, but he showed the kids God by teaching them things about geology, history, and His physical creation. The ideal I had in my head kept me from appreciating his unique contribution.

Does it surprise you to know that every kind of pain and heartache that exists in those who are unchurched is also found in those who are churched? Many Christians are hurting even though they're redeemed. We're in process, not finished works, but we can be confident that "he who began a good work in [us] will carry it on to completion until the day of Christ Jesus" (Phil. 1:6).

THE IDEAL SELF

You have an "ideal self" in your head. It's a picture of the person you want to be, think you should be, and need to be in order to feel OK with yourself. When your real self differs from your ideal self, you judge yourself. The ideal self contains the messages from your parents and significant others. This "critical parent" that resides in your mind consists partially of the things you were told to do and be.

Ted's father was a scientist. Ted had trouble with science and math throughout school, and his father was critical and impatient with him because of it. Today, Ted is a successful carpenter, but he still compares himself to his father. He says, "I know I have low self-esteem. I feel like a failure. In my mind I can be a success only if I'm good at math and science like my father." Ted's ideal is to be like his father; anything less falls short.

Karen's ideal self is that of a stay-at-home mom who home-schools her children. She feels badly about herself because she lacks the patience to teach them, is not a great cook, and feels her house is not well-organized. She compares herself to her own mother and to friends who fit her ideal.

Ronda's ideal was to be always in control of her emotions and never appear weak. When she lost control or needed help, she berated herself. She also believed that relationships should be without conflicts. When she and her husband argued, she felt like a failure.

The critical voice in your head tells you things such as "You should be happy." "You should work hard." "You should be strong." "You should sacrifice for others." "You should be a bigger success." "You should _____." (Fill in the blank with your own "should.") This often masquerades as perfectionism, where the standards we set for ourselves are impossible to reach. Ironically, perfectionism is driven by a fear of failure even though it actually ensures we'll see ourselves as failures. God doesn't want us to be driven by fear, because "perfect love drives out fear, because fear has to do with punishment" (1 John 4:18). Perfectionists feel they have to be perfect in order to be loved and accepted. No one can meet the expectations of his or her ideal self. Anytime we measure our real selves against our ideal selves, we feel like failures.

You may go to the other extreme and not try at all because you fear failure. You may not try new things or take risks, and you may even step back from doing what you are competent in. *After all*, you reason, *if I'm going to fail, why risk trying? I'll only end up feeling worse about myself when I go through another letdown.*

Once you view yourself as a worthless failure, you'll find ways to prove it. Matt felt insecure at work. He focused on his mistakes, the coworkers who did better than he, and his boss's criticism. The more insecure he felt, the worse he seemed to do. The more you focus on the negatives, the worse you'll feel about yourself and the more you'll believe you really are inadequate. Are you ever really a failure? Being a failure would mean you can't do anything right. That's not possible. You're able to do some things right and are good and competent at something. The problem comes when your ideal self doesn't value those things.

Even if you've failed in the past, that doesn't mean you're a failure today, nor does it mean you're worthless. Many people try for a long time before succeeding at something. No matter what it is— failing with your diet, failing to control your anger, failing an exam, failing to beat an addiction, or failing at sexual purity—past failures don't have to predict future failures.

Pursuing excellence and pursuing perfect performance are two different things. When pursuing excellence, you expect to make mistakes and learn from them and enjoy the pursuit of your goal. You see a mistake as a "missed take." You know you get as many replays as you need. With perfectionism, the drive you feel to succeed might not even correlate with what you enjoy. As in Ted's case, his ideal self was to be like his father, but that wasn't who he was. He probably would have hated being a scientist anyway.

Your ideal self is full of "shoulds" and "oughts," both of which put you in bondage. Kathy experienced that bondage. "I can never relax and be satisfied. It's as if there's a voice in my head telling me to do better, be more, get more, try harder. It feels as if it's God's voice." God doesn't want Kathy or you in bondage to an image. "It is for freedom that Christ has set us free. Stand firm, then, and do not let yourselves be burdened again by a yoke of slavery" (Gal. 5:1). The legalism of dos and don'ts is a losing proposition; it's the opposite of grace (Gal. 5:4). Ideals are good motivators but should not be rigid laws against which you measure yourself and condemn yourself. God wants you to embrace His image of you by discovering your real image and letting go of your legalistic ideal image.

If we grasp God's view of our value and beauty, we can be set free from our limited view that we're only as valuable as our appearance, wealth, and abilities. When I meditate on how God sees me, I feel loved, accepted, and perfected.

How do *you* feel? Will you exchange your reflected image for the image God has of you?

QUESTIONS FOR REFLECTION

1. Describe your ideal man and woman. How does comparing yourself to this image affect you?

2. Do you compare your spouse or children to an ideal image? How does that affect your view of them and your relationships with them?

3. How would focusing on your inner beauty rather than your outer beauty or your possessions change your image of yourself and your life?

4. Do you have physical attributes that are hard for you to accept? How has your unwillingness to accept them affected your self-image?

5. How would comparing yourself only against yourself change your self-image?

6. What is your image of the ideal Christian, husband, wife, and parent? How does holding these images bring discouragement into your life and relationships?

7. Describe your ideal self. How does it differ from your real self?

8. Name some of the "shoulds" you have in your head. Are they realistic?

9. How do you deal with a less-than-perfect performance?

10. Meditate on scripture that helps you see yourself as God sees you. Does this affect your image of yourself?

5

STAINED

images

*"COME NOW, LET US REASON
TOGETHER," SAYS THE LORD,
"THOUGH YOUR SINS ARE LIKE SCARLET,
THEY SHALL BE AS WHITE AS SNOW;
THOUGH THEY ARE RED AS CRIMSON,
THEY SHALL BE LIKE WOOL."*
—ISA. 1:18

5

STAINED
images

"COME NOW, LET US REASON
TOGETHER," SAYS THE LORD,
"THOUGH YOUR SINS ARE LIKE SCARLET,
THEY SHALL BE AS WHITE AS SNOW;
THOUGH THEY ARE RED AS CRIMSON,
THEY SHALL BE LIKE WOOL."
—ISA. 1:18

All of us have regrets for things we have done or not done, for missed opportunities, mistakes, failures, or harm we have done to others. Some regrets are very painful and some less painful. Part of self-image comes from how we view ourselves in light of the past. In order to hold a real self-image, we must deal with the past correctly so we can view it in true perspective and not allow it to stain our self-image today.

It's important to assess your past and honestly admit the things you've done or not done that you now regret. The purpose isn't to beat yourself up but to gain understanding, take responsibility, and change the way you live today and to keep you from being weighted down by the negative emotions associated with guilt.

SPECIFIC REGRETS

It's easy to look at the past and see now what would have been wiser choices. You're older and wiser now and have information you didn't have then. At the time, you may have been limited by your circumstances, abilities, experience, age, and incomplete knowledge and awareness. As you consider your regrets, try to gain understanding by answering these questions:

- What were the circumstances and pressures?
- What was I thinking and feeling at the time?
- What was my self-image, including my self-esteem and self-worth, at the time?
- What support did I have from people around me?
- What would I say to someone in the same circumstances who did the same thing? Can I extend the same grace and acceptance to myself?

CHILDHOOD CHOICES

Many of us made foolish and impulsive decisions, especially as teenagers. When you were a teen, did you think you had all the answers and that your parents were stupid? I did. In retrospect, though, I made some pretty bad choices.

Remember—you had only partial awareness as a child; you can't hold yourself to the same standard that you do today as an adult (1 Cor. 13:11). Parker can't believe he made the stupid choices regarding drug use that he made in high school. Royce is amazed when he reflects on his poor grades and bad attitude toward his parents and their values. Faye feels embarrassed when she thinks of the scanty clothes she wore as a teen.

As a teen, you were vulnerable to inside and outside pressures that you didn't have the maturity to handle: peer pressure, societal norms, hormones, body changes, and dysfunctional family dynamics.

SEXUAL CHOICES

Many people have regrets about choices they made sexually. Maybe you had sex before you were married, were involved in an affair, or used pornography. Even though the world tells us that promiscuity is normal and acceptable, it takes a huge toll on us emotionally, spiritually, and even physically. God created sex to be more than a physical union—it's a spiritual union also. When we commit sexual sins, we sin against our own bodies and the Lord (1 Cor. 6:16-20).

Memories associated with sexuality are strong and deeply encoded in our brains. We feel powerful emotions: shame, remorse, embarrassment, rejection, and anger. Many of us had such low self-esteem that any positive attention from the opposite sex felt like validation. Nora believed she was nothing unless a guy liked her, so she did anything she could to have a boyfriend—including sexual promiscuity at age 13. She now sees how she devalued herself. She didn't have the emotional maturity to understand that some types of attention aren't validating—they're insulting. Maybe you fell for the lie that you're nothing unless you have a boyfriend or girlfriend. Sometimes a woman believes that a man's sexual interest means she's loved. A man will sometimes believe that if a woman allows him to do things for her, it means she cares about him. Afterwards, a person may feel used, realizing that it wasn't love but lust or convenience.

EDUCATIONAL AND VOCATIONAL CHOICES

Educational choices and vocational choices include the decisions you made regarding how hard you tried in school, whether you attended and finished college or trained for a particular vocation or career.

Regrets about missed opportunities can be devastating or mild, depending on your circumstances. As you look back at the choices you now regret, try to remember what your reasons were at the time:

- Were your financial resources or opportunities limited?
- Was your self-esteem so low that you didn't think you could succeed?
- Was your family negative or supportive concerning your goals?
- Were you uncertain about the direction you wanted to pursue?

- Were you struggling with other things that appeared to be more important at the time?
- Were your goals limited compared to what you've grown to see yourself capable of now? Were you not interested in the same things then?

Answering these questions can help you come to terms with the decisions you made. Life experiences change and enlarge you, and you may be a different person today than you were before. While you can't change the choices you made in the past, you can ask yourself, *Is there a goal that I can begin to pursue now?* If you want a change but aren't sure of what you want to do, begin to assess your strengths and weaknesses. Answer the following questions:

- What do I prefer to do above everything else?
- What makes me nervous and stressed? (Which means *I don't want to do this.*)
- What do people compliment me on?
- Am I a people person, or do I prefer to work away from people?
- Do I like to sit still or move around? Would I prefer to work indoors or out?
- What are my natural skills and talents?
- What in my past work or life experience would prepare me for a new vocation?
- If I had my dream life or job, what would it be?

Allow your mind to wander as you answer these questions. You may not be able to do exactly what you dream of due to real-life constraints like geographic location, health, physical ability, opportunity, age, and family responsibilities, but break down the components and see what the possibilities are.

It's never too late to go back to school or pursue a new vocation. There are many opportunities to improve your skills. You may not be able to devote yourself to new training full-time due to adult responsibilities, but you can set some goals and do it slowly, even if it takes a long time. The time will pass anyway, whether you pursue your goal or not.

If you aren't able to pursue a new profession or college degree, you may still be able to do something in that field or with that ability. Maybe it won't be through a career but through volunteer work that affirms you and uses your skills, talents, and experiences.

For instance, if you realize you should have been a teacher but realize that going to college full-time for four or more years or part-time for even longer is impossible, then look for other opportunities to teach. Maybe you have a skill you could teach others, like sewing, cake-decorating, or drawing. Maybe you could teach English as a second language at a night school or tutor children having difficulty in school. Maybe you could get a job as a teacher's aide or teach preschool, neither of which require a college degree. You could even teach a Bible study or Sunday School class. If it's too late to be a doctor, you may want to pursue something else in the medical field that requires less training, such as X-ray technician work. If you wanted to be a nurse, it may be because you love caring for people. There are many ways you can do that if you can't pursue a nursing career. You could be a part of your church's care ministry, visiting the sick, or be a caregiver for disabled people.

Acknowledge your regrets, see what you naturally like to do, and find a way to turn those regrets into something positive today. It's a guaranteed self-worth and self-esteem booster. Doing something you love brings out the best in you and increases your satisfaction with the person God created you to be.

RELATIONSHIP CHOICES

Relationship regrets can feel overwhelming. It is key to realize that a relationship is made up of two people: you and the other person. Both of you bring your pasts, temperaments, strengths, and weaknesses into the relationship. You create a mutual dynamic together, and each of you affects the other. Therefore, both of you are responsible for the success or failure, even though the percentage isn't always 50/50. When you look back in hindsight and wish you had done things differently, you're looking through the lens you have today, not the one you had before.

Elena was still processing whose fault the divorce was three years later. She would go through periods of blaming herself entirely and regretted not making certain changes. Other times, she blamed her former husband completely. Elena needs to accept that both she and her husband were partially to blame and that she did the best she could at the time.

Relationship difficulties are painful growth experiences, especially if it involves rejection by someone you loved or wanted a relationship with. Your self-esteem can be devastated, particularly if you conclude that you're unlovable. Just because you were unable to make it work with one person, or one person rejected you for whatever his or her personal reasons were, it doesn't make you a failure. It didn't work for lots of complicated reasons that became bigger than the two of you could handle. Admit your part, let the other person be responsible for his or her part, accept that you did the best you could at the time, and let it go. It doesn't have to define who you are today. How you view yourself has huge implications for your self-image.

If you've lived long enough, you have relationship regrets. We all do. In hindsight, you may wish you had made some different choices. Join the club. Whatever you regret, identify it, admit it, and if you can make a change today, do it. If you can't, let it go.

PARENTAL CHOICES

Parents want what's best for their children. Jesus referred to this when He said, "Which of you, if his son asks for bread, will give him a stone? Or if he asks for a fish, will give him a snake?" (Matt. 7:9-10). The implication is that no one would.

Children don't come with manuals. They're little people with individual personalities and temperaments. Each child reacts differently to the same parents, and parents react differently to each child as the personality of the parent and child mix together to form a dynamic specific to the two of them. Children aren't always easy, and it's impossible not to make a mistake in 18 years. As parents, we learn as we go and are typically harder on firstborns and easier on younger children.

It's normal to look back on children who had academic, emotional, medical, or behavioral problems and see that you made mistakes because of the additional challenges these difficulties bring. Maybe you didn't recognize the problems early enough or missed them entirely. Maybe you overlooked treatments that you now believe would have helped. Maybe you disciplined problems because you thought the misbehavior was purposeful and now know it was caused by something else. Maybe you have regrets about being impatient. You may also have regrets about not developing a talent in a child.

I can look back in hindsight and see the mistakes I made with my children. Some of the mistakes were well intentioned; I thought I was doing right at the time. One of my daughters was particularly strong-willed. I thought the right choice was to make her back down, but it didn't work. I can see now that a gentler approach such as using logical consequences would have been better, but it's too late to go back and do it a different way.

Maybe you raised your children with a one-size-fits-all formula and now realize that the temperament of each child requires a tailor-made formula for discipline. Maybe legitimate challenges such as illness, employment, marital problems, or other demands caused you to be emotionally or physically unavailable for your children. Maybe you had addictions or other problems that interfered with your ability to parent.

Take responsibility for the things you did that affected your children negatively. You may decide to apologize to them, but you don't have to beat yourself up forever or enable your children to make bad choices now or allow them to mistreat you because you feel guilty. That isn't in their best interest—or yours. Yes, you affected them. And if part of your amends is to help them through counseling to get insight into their problems, you can do that. But if they're now adults, the responsibility for making right choices—in spite of everything you did or didn't do—becomes theirs today.

Some children raised in good homes make bad choices, and some children raised in bad homes make good choices. Children are born with a sin nature and choose to do wrong. Yes, wounds from childhood contribute to emotional problems and bad choices, but even then, the choice is the child's.

Marty was consumed with guilt over her daughter's choice to

use drugs and move in with her boyfriend. Marty was convinced that her divorce from Janna's father and the problems in the home caused Janna to turn to drugs. Yet Marty had three other children, one older than Janna, who didn't make that choice. Marty must accept that even though Janna's childhood wasn't perfect and the divorce was painful, Janna still made her own choices and could have chosen a different path.

FINANCIAL CHOICES

Financial wealth and material possessions are often equated with success. Rich people are admired and revered. The converse is also true. Poor people are determined to have less value and are often shunned. The apostle James dealt with a similar situation in his church (James 2:1-8). The people were showing favoritism to the rich by offering them the best seats. James reminded them that God favors the poor over the rich.

If you had a financial dream that you haven't achieved, you may feel you've failed. That may not be the case. Maybe your dream was unrealistic. Maybe you did the best you could, and circumstances arose that prevented you from reaching that goal. Your dream may need a reality adjustment that redefines it to fit the actual circumstances of your life. That was Ben's situation. He dreamed of owning a real estate office and having agents work for him. That didn't happen, but he was a successful real estate agent and could readjust his dream and feel good about it.

You may have specific financial regrets that you must come to terms with. Perhaps you should make amends directly to someone by repaying money you've borrowed. Or perhaps you must come to terms with a financial loss due to poor decisions made with good intentions such as investments that didn't turn out well. Investing isn't foolproof, and there's always a chance of success or failure. If you need guidance in these matters, get help from a financial advisor and begin to make changes to ensure a better future.

SPIRITUAL CHOICES

Perhaps you regret your spiritual choices. Maybe you wasted years when you could have been serving the Lord, or you served out of compulsion rather than love. Maybe you were a Christian but bore little fruit because you were overly focused on the cares of the world (Matt. 13:22). You may have made bad choices that brought disrepute to His name and caused others to stumble.

Regardless of what you've done in the past, God is always ready to forgive and welcome back His prodigal children with open arms (Luke 15:11-32). It's never too late to begin serving the Lord completely with your heart, soul, and mind (Matt. 22:37).

UNDERSTANDING GUILT AND SHAME

Hebrews 12:1 says, "Let us throw off everything that hinders and the sin that so easily entangles, and let us run with perseverance the race marked out for us." Unless the past is properly dealt with, it hinders us in running our race by holding us back and weighs us down with guilt, shame, self-pity, low self-esteem, low self-worth, and the need to cover up and hide.

The cycle of addiction or habitual sin involves the following: acting out or engaging in the addiction or sin, feeling guilty and shameful about acting out, feeling low self-worth and low self-esteem and then acting out again to temporarily rid oneself of the negative feelings. Thus, the shame and low self-esteem contribute to the choice to continue engaging in the addiction or sin. Unwill-ingness to face the responsibility for the addiction or behavior also contributes to the need to hide and cover up the act and blame it on other people.

Guilt is feeling badly about *what we do*; shame is feeling bad-ly about *who we are*. A person with a wrong self-image easily feels shame. Shame condemns and passes judgment. It makes you feel that because of what you did, you're no good or are incapable of change. When you're stuck in shame, it's difficult to admit what you did wrong, because the admission makes you feel worthless. It con-firms your fear that you're as bad as you fear you are. Unconfessed sin grows into shame, because the more you hide the truth and fear admitting it, the worse you feel about yourself, and the more sepa-rated from God you feel. That heaviness results in your believing that you're incapable of being forgiven and redeemed from your mistake. You lose hope.

Shame can hold you back from doing the things you want to do but lack the confidence to do. A self-image stained by shame prevents you from believing you can succeed or change, because you can't see yourself differently than you are or have been. Para-doxically, the more you want to change, the worse you feel about yourself for not changing.

A person with low self-esteem doesn't process his or her mis-takes and grow from them. The process is short-circuited and goes like this: "I did a bad thing; therefore, I'm bad. I'm hopelessly flawed and unworthy. I feel badly about what I did *and* about my-self." God does want us to feel badly enough to repent and be set free to do better the next time. The blessing of forgiveness is a clean slate that allows you to effectively start over with that white robe of the righteousness of the Lord (Rev. 3:18; 6:11).

KING DAVID'S EXAMPLE

David was a man after God's own heart, yet even he fell into sin. In 2 Sam. 11—12 we're provided with a perfect example of how sin blinds us and how becoming accountable sets us free from the past.

One of David's perks as king was that he had many wives and concubines. But he still wasn't satisfied. When he saw the beautiful Bathsheba bathing, he decided that he wanted her. Their adultery resulted in her becoming pregnant, and David's solution was to fix the problem through more deception. He arranged for her husband, Uriah, to come home from battle so he would sleep with his wife and therefore believe he fathered the child. But Uriah had too much integrity to enjoy pleasure while his fellow soldiers were risking their lives in combat, so he refused to sleep with Bathsheba. David continued his scheme to cover his sin by concocting a plan to put Uriah in the front lines of battle alone where he would be killed. It worked. David then married Bathsheba. From all the evidence in Scripture, David didn't appear to be convicted through this process. But God was very displeased.

God sent Nathan to tell David this story: A poor man had one lamb. He loved it and cherished it. It was more like a daughter to him than an animal for food. A rich man with many sheep and cattle came into town and took the man's lamb, killed it, and ate it rather than taking one of his own.

Upon hearing this story, David became angry, readily recognizing the injustice of the situation. He demanded the man make restitution by repaying the lamb's owner four times what the lamb was worth and maybe even giving up his life. Nathan confronted David with the truth: David was just like this man. He had taken another man's wife, even though he had many wives of his own, and even killed the other man.

David was at a crossroads. He could deal with his past or hide from it. He could have thrown Nathan out, had him killed, or argued with him. He could have continued to excuse his sin, cover it up, or even blame Bathsheba. Instead, he recognized his sin and admitted it.

Nathan immediately reassured David that God had already forgiven his sin but that there would be consequences. David's family would be split, fighting against each other, and one of his sons would do the same to him by sleeping with David's wives. And the baby Bathsheba was carrying would die.

David dealt with his sin. After admitting it, he began to do what he could to rectify the situation. He prayed and fasted, asking God to spare the child. His servants were so worried about him that when the child actually died, they were afraid to tell him, because they thought his reaction might be worse. They were surprised, because after they told him, he came out of the room and returned to his normal duties. In response to their questions, David told them that he had to try to prevent the child's death. But after it was done, he had to accept it and continue to live his life.

LETTING GO

David's story gives us a perfect picture of dealing with mistakes and regrets.

1. After becoming aware of what you have done, admit your fault.

2. Do what you can to rectify the situation.

3. Face the consequences.

4. Let it go and live your life.

As we mature in our faith and knowledge of the Bible, we become more attuned to right and wrong. There are times we may not know we've done wrong until later. We must be accountable for our sins when we recognize them (Lev. 4:13-14, 22-23, 27-28). Other times, we know we're doing something wrong, and we don't want to do it, but we do it anyway (Rom. 7:19). The third possibility is that our hearts are hardened by repeatedly sinning (Heb. 3:13), and we don't even care. Whatever the reasons for making what we now recognize as a wrong choice, we must deal with it in the same way, using David's process.

Sometimes the consequences of sin affect only us, but at other times they affect other people. Living with the awareness that your actions have caused others to suffer can easily lead to discouragement unless you do what you can and then let it go, as David did. Sometimes holding on to guilt can lead us to do things that prevent others from being responsible for themselves, which further harms them. Even if your actions have hurt others, you can't fix it for them. Admit what you did, make appropriate restitution, and then continue to lead your life and allow others to lead theirs. God is not limited by your mistakes; what you did wrong can still be used for good by God (Gen. 50:20) in your life and in the lives of others. When you become accountable for your mistakes, others might not be ready to let it go right away. Give them the time and space they need to heal. The best way you can show someone you're sorry is to be different. This "living amends" is a powerful testimony to the fact that you truly are repentant.

We reap what we sow, so there will be consequences to our choices (Gal. 6:7-8).

Sal led a sexually promiscuous lifestyle and used drugs until he was diagnosed with HIV, which brought him back to the Lord. He was a powerful example of David's process. Sal realized that his actions led to his illness. He apologized to the people he hurt along the way and began to treat them differently. He didn't blame God or others and lived each day fully by reaching out to others and testifying to God's mercy and grace. From the day he was diagnosed until the day he died, he lived in the present rather than the past.

Forgiving yourself is part of getting on with your life. You accept that, for whatever reasons, you did what you did, and it was the best you could do at the time. You can't change it; regrets about what never was and never will be are futile. Your only option is to live today and go forward (Phil. 3:13). The purpose of looking at your past is to "strengthen your feeble arms and weak knees . . . so that the lame may not be disabled, but rather healed" (Heb. 12:12-13). Looking at your past is meant to *encourage* rather than discourage you.

God has redeemed you in spite of your past and has made you perfect in Him. There are no big sins and little sins in God's eyes, only in ours. The apostle Paul said,

> Even though I was once a blasphemer and a persecutor and a violent man, I was shown mercy because I acted in ignorance and unbelief. . . . Christ Jesus came into the world to save sinners—of whom I am the worst. But for that very reason I was shown mercy so that in me, the worst of sinners, Christ Jesus might display his unlimited patience as an example for those who would believe on him and receive eternal life (*1 Tim. 1:13, 15-16*).

No mistake or sin or missed opportunity is bigger than God's ability to turn it around for your good and His glory (Rom. 8:28). Making a mistake is not the same as *being* a mistake. God works everything for His purpose, even the things we do wrong (Prov. 16:4).

You can exchange your stained image for a clean image. (See Isa. 1:18).

QUESTIONS FOR REFLECTION

1. What are some of your childhood regrets?

2. What are some of your sexual regrets?

3. What are some of your educational and vocational regrets?

4. What are some of your relationship regrets?

5. What are some of your parenting regrets?

6. What are some of your financial regrets?

7. What are some of your spiritual regrets?

8. How do guilt and shame affect your life and your ability to change yourself?

9. Can you let go of your regrets? What helps you let go and live? What holds you back from letting go?

10. What changes can you make today so you'll have fewer regrets tomorrow?

6

FALSE

images

EACH OF YOU MUST PUT OFF
FALSEHOOD AND SPEAK TRUTHFULLY
TO HIS NEIGHBOR.
—EPH. 4:25

6

FALSE

images

EACH OF YOU MUST PUT OFF
FALSEHOOD AND SPEAK TRUTHFULLY
TO HIS NEIGHBOR.
—EPH. 4:25

A false image is an image that's not real or truthful. It can originate from pain, fear, pride, inadequacy, deception, denial, pretending, or defensiveness. A false image can be protective or deliberately deceptive. Defensiveness stems from an inability to face the truth. Arrogance and conceit present an overly positive image to counter a deep sense of inferiority. Covering up is often a way of avoiding pain. Some hide behind the mask of achievements to prove their worth. Adjusting one's image to please others stems from the need for approval. False images are the opposite of living in truth, and they result in captivity and bondage.

MASKING YOUR NAKEDNESS

Adam and Eve were created perfect. In their perfection they were transparent and comfortable with being themselves. After they sinned, they became aware of their inadequacies and nakedness and instinctively ran for cover by hiding, denying, blaming, and lying. God understood their new need for a covering and made them clothing from animal skins. This symbolic mask hid their nakedness. We, too, wear masks to cover our vulnerabilities and nakedness. We don't want people to see that we're weak, insecure, fallible, and filled with self-doubt. We pretend we have it all together so we don't risk rejection and losing the connection with God and others that we so desperately need.

When you let your guard down and someone hurts you, you may react by putting on your mask the next time. You may say to yourself, *I'll never be open again. I'm not going to let anyone have a chance to reject me.* Your fear of further rejection makes it feel safer to hide.

George was laughed at in grade school when he didn't do

well at sports. He vowed he would not fail in front of others again and would not let others know he was hurt by their rejection.

Dayna was embarrassed by her father's alcoholism and her parents arguing in front of her friends. She vowed she would never do anything to cause her to be ashamed.

Vicky acts tough and sarcastic with people. She finally admitted that it's easier to cause people to dislike her because she's rude than to show her real self and be rejected.

Tara told her husband that his jokes about her weight hurt her feelings, but he dismissed her concerns. She decided to pretend the comments didn't bother her and began to joke about her weight herself.

George, Dayna, Vicky, and Tara put on false images to mask their nakedness and vulnerability.

COVERING YOUR PAIN

You carry a degree of emotional pain related to wounds from imperfect people, broken relationships, unfulfilled dreams, and failed expectations. You may put on a variety of masks to cover the pain so no one will see what's really inside. The "I don't need anybody" mask prevents you from being hurt again. The "I'm not capable" mask is worn to protect you from having to risk trying and failing.

The "I'm fine" mask keeps you from having to share your inner secrets and risk being vulnerable. The "I don't have any problems" mask allows you to hide behind a lie so you don't have to face the truth about your life. The "I don't deserve good things" mask protects you from having to face loss. The "I don't care about anything" mask keeps you from being disappointed again. The "I'm in control" mask keeps you from letting people see your emotions and your spontaneous side for fear of being rejected. The "I'm always right" mask keeps you from having to admit that you don't know everything and risking disapproval or loss of respect in the person's eyes. We don't wear one mask all the time; we switch, depending on the situation we're in and who we're with.

When you show your true feelings or do what feels right and are validated and accepted by others, you naturally embrace those parts of yourself. But when you receive disapproval or experience pain as a result of being yourself, you naturally want to deny those parts of yourself. Tasha's mom repeatedly said, "Nice girls don't get angry," so Tasha began to deny that she was angry and pretended everything was OK. Today she finds herself passively resisting her husband and children, but she denies that she's angry.

Jason's dad was a tough guy and not afraid of anything. From the time Jason was a little boy, his dad reprimanded him for being afraid. Jason hides his anxiety and fear as an adult, acts tough, and doesn't let anyone know he's filled with insecurities.

Subtle invalidation occurs when people reward some behaviors and characteristics but ignore others. If people embrace and accept only your positive parts, you'll tend to feel badly about the negative parts of yourself and hide them. This is especially true for children who are forming their self-images. For instance, if a child can't show fear without being shamed, he or she will push the anxiety inward and pretend he or she is not afraid of anything. This overcompensation results in a false sense of self. Yet when the parents embrace the positive and negative emotions and behavior and address them both forthrightly and honestly, the child receives feedback that says, "I can be me, experience both good and bad feelings, and still be OK." Both parts of self are integrated and accepted.

Some of us have such a good cover that others don't know what's really going on inside us. The rest of us think we're doing a good job at covering it up—but people know something's wrong.

DEFENDING YOUR BROKENNESS

Defenses are cover-ups for feelings of inadequacy, weakness, fear, and insecurity. They protect us from perceived threats and allow us to maintain false images. We all use them some of the time, but when used too much, they're unhealthy.

We use defenses to protect ourselves from facing the truth about ourselves or admitting it to others. When Cain was confronted with the fact that God wasn't happy with his sacrifice of fruit, he got defensive. Instead of looking within himself and seeing what he could do to correct the situation, he blamed Abel and solved his dilemma by killing him. God warned Cain that he was about to make a big mistake, but Cain wasn't willing to face the truth about himself (Gen. 4:2-8). Cain is a perfect example of this defensive filter. When we refuse to look at ourselves and introspectively analyze what we're doing, we'll do things that are unhealthy and destructive, even though they may feel right at the time. Instead, our prayer should be that of the blind men in Matt. 20:30-33 who cried out to Jesus to open their eyes.

Pat had a controlling and abusive father who didn't allow him to express his feelings and was very harsh with him when he made a mistake, even ridiculing him in front of his friends. Pat's wife, Kim, complains that she can't talk to Pat about her feelings or problems between them, because he instantly reacts by getting angry and denying the problem or by saying she's accusing him of being a terrible husband. Kim is frustrated and angry. "He's so defensive. He never admits he's wrong, and he turns it all back on me every time I bring up an issue. It's impossible to get through to him."

Pat is protecting himself. Kim's criticisms expose his fears that he really isn't OK. He reacts to her angrily to keep her from exposing his weaknesses. If he does allow himself to entertain the thought that she might have a valid criticism, he feels overwhelmed by it. He denies it and continues to see himself as right and her as wrong.

Denial is another defense from pain. Marge couldn't accept that her son was using drugs, so she refused to admit it or deal with it. Hal couldn't admit that he needed help with his depression. Denial often has to just run its course. One won't face things until he or she is ready.

Another defense is rationalization or justification, which is nothing more than offering excuses for doing something you don't want to take responsibility for. Tammy procrastinated paying the monthly bills. When John confronted her over the late charges, she gave him a long list of all the reasons she didn't do it. John was frustrated. Tammy could have paid the bills, and he knew it.

Justification and rationalization prevent us from having to risk stating the truth about something we did because we fear the consequences or the prospect that someone will think badly about us. Blame accomplishes the same thing but pushes the responsibility onto someone else. Ultimately, covering sin and brokenness doesn't work; rather than making us prosper, it keeps us stuck and unable to move forward in truth (Ps. 32).

PROVING YOUR WORTH

One of the ways we react to a deep feeling of unworthiness is to try to prove our worth. One of the most common ways to do this is to attempt to do something upon which to build an image. Our list of accomplishments becomes our false mask. Our society is steeped in the work ethic, and we place a premium on work. Work is good and necessary and pleasing to God. The apostle Paul said that if a man didn't work he shouldn't eat (2 Thess. 3:10). God wants our faith to be backed up by works (James 1:22). Adam was given the task of tending the Garden of Eden even before the Fall (Gen. 2:15). Society will reward us for our efforts with a paycheck, accolades, and material goods. Accomplishments aren't wrong, but if they're linked to overall worth and we lose them, we may feel discouraged and worthless. Our ultimate worth is not dependent on what we do.

Some personalities are naturally more driven than others. The type A personality is achievement-oriented and pushes hard to do more and more. The type B personality may accomplish as much but at a more relaxed pace. I've been told that I'm a type AAA. Since I value productivity, I become frustrated if I feel time is wasted and I haven't accomplished anything. I also feel frustrated by little things that don't feel worthwhile to me.

Understanding this helps me accept myself and work within my strengths and weaknesses. I enjoy my natural drive but must make sure I don't equate productivity with worth. I have to ask myself, *If I didn't have accomplishments and couldn't be productive, would I still know I'm valuable? Do I value others if they don't accomplish as much? Do I recognize that what I do doesn't make me any more valuable to God?*

EXALTING YOUR ABILITIES

Conceit is an excessively favorable view of oneself, and conceit is linked to arrogance. Arrogance is a display of excessive superiority that flaunts itself. Underneath arrogance lies haughtiness or snobbery. You can easily see how that attitude is the opposite of Christ's, who never flaunted His true nature but instead gave it up completely and made himself a servant even to those who mistreated and disliked Him (Phil. 2:6-8).

Contrast Christ's attitude with Satan's arrogance. Satan was beautiful and superior to the other angels, but he had an excessively favorable view of himself, thinking he was capable of equality with God. He arrogantly asserted himself, which resulted in his fall and expulsion from heaven (Isa. 14:12-15). God says He hates pride and arrogance as much as any other evil (Prov. 8:12-13). He warns us not to become conceited, thinking we're more than we are (Gal. 6:3; Rom. 12:3), so that we won't fall under the same judgment as Satan (1 Tim. 3:6).

Arrogant people have attitudes of superiority, but in reality, they're fearful, insecure, and feel inferior. The mask of superiority is their cover-up. They act proud and boastful, invite admiration and praise, and refuse to admit their weaknesses out of fear. They may even be covering up the truth of their inferiority from themselves. Taking off the mask and admitting their flaws is too scary, so they wear a mask that projects the opposite: overconfidence.

Cameron was an arrogant guy. He drove a fancy car, revved the engine loudly, dressed with expensive name-brand clothes, talked about how much money he made, and bragged about his famous contacts. Everyone thought he was arrogant, but his wife knew that inside he was a little boy who craved approval and doubted himself.

The Pharisees maintained a hypocritical false image. On the outside they appeared to be "super-righteous," but on the inside they were full of things that didn't match their exterior (Matt. 23:27-28). They kept some parts of the law but didn't value the more important things like justice, mercy, and faithfulness (Matt. 23:23). Their righteousness didn't come from admitting their brokenness and need for God but through their external appearances and acts. They cared only about what people thought about them and wanted praise from others (Matt. 23:5-7). Keeping outward regulations has an appearance of humility but in reality doesn't have any value at all (Col. 2:20-23). If you need to flaunt your righteousness, you'll wear a false image that denies the parts of yourself that aren't perfect, and you won't be able to be real or grow in your relationships with God and others.

ADJUSTING YOUR IMAGE

Are you comfortable with who you are? Or do you adjust your image to be what others want you to be? All of us succumb to people-pleasing once in a while when the pressure is on, but some of us are so afraid to be ourselves that we develop a radar sense at figuring out what people want and automatically adjust ourselves to it.

If you need the approval of other people, you'll find yourself adjusting your image to fit what you think they want you to be. But there are some faulty assumptions underlying this need for approval. Here are some of the faulty beliefs people-pleasers hold:

- You *have* to please other people.
- If you have the approval of people, you'll be happy.

- Others will like you more if you're the kind of person they want you to be.
- If you let people see the real you, they won't like you.
- Your needs are less important than the needs of others.
- You can't endure disapproval or rejection; it's just too much to handle.
- Your self-worth and value depend on the opinions of others.
- If someone doesn't like you, it's because there's something wrong with you.

These beliefs are fundamentally wrong. The truth is—

- You don't have to please other people—it's your choice.
- You can be happy even if others don't approve of you, like you, or agree with you.
- People might like the real you more than the false you.
- People might like you more if you're vulnerable and let them see who you really are.
- Both your needs and the needs of others are important.
- You can endure disapproval and rejection. It's uncomfortable, but you'll survive.
- Your self-worth and value don't depend on the opinions of other people.
- Not everyone will like you, and that doesn't mean there's something wrong with you. You don't like everyone else either.
- You don't have to please everyone—only God and yourself.

Jesus wasn't dependent on anyone's approval except His Father's (John 6:38). Good thing, too, because more people hated Him than liked Him. They called Him names, doubted His teaching and claims (John 10:22-33), accused Him of driving out demons by Satan's power and of being demon-possessed (Luke 11:14-15; John 8:48), tried to set Him up with trick questions (Matt. 19:3; 22:15), and plotted to kill Him (Matt. 26:3-4).

Jesus did many things that others thought were wrong: He associated with Samaritans (John 4:7-9), ate with sinners and tax collectors (Matt. 9:9-13), healed on the Sabbath (John 5:16), stayed at the Temple without His parents' approval (Luke 2:41-50), claimed to be equal with God (John 5:17-18), and rebuked the religious leaders (Matt. 23:13-32). When Jesus followed His convictions, many people were unhappy with Him. Yet He stood firm, because His self-worth came from pleasing God, not other people. He knew who He was and didn't need to hide behind a false image. He endured the rejection of people, because He knew He was chosen by God and was precious to His Father (1 Pet. 2:4).

Jesus warned us that we wouldn't be approved by the world either (John 15:18-20). In fact, He went so far as to say in Luke 6:26 that if everyone liked you and spoke well of you, you had to be doing something wrong!

Adjusting your mask to fit what you think others want you to be doesn't work. When you desperately need the approval of others, you're setting yourself up to fail. When you base your self-worth on the opinions and views of others, you're getting approval for being something you aren't. So even their positive response to you won't erase the deep inward belief that the "real you" is still inadequate.

When you adjust your image to please others, you focus on your outside image and ignore your inside image. God cares more about what's inside you than outside (Matt. 15:10). If your motive is to be seen by people to get their approval, your motive is wrong

(Matt. 6:1-6). The key to Jesus' ability to be who He was and not be swayed by others was that He didn't pay attention to who they were (Matt. 22:16). He wasn't impressed or influenced by position or title and didn't compare himself to others. When we compare ourselves to others, we'll be more likely to need their approval.

Kelly was convinced she wasn't doing a good job at work, because her boss criticized her work and never complimented her. The truth was that he was a difficult person to deal with and didn't compliment *any* of his employees. Kelly felt better when she accepted the fact that she wouldn't get his approval.

Hank's wife didn't understand or approve of his conversion to Christianity. It was hard, but he had to accept that he would have to live with her disapproval of his faith.

Larry had two lives: one with his church friends and another with his worldly friends. Saying no to the things his worldly friends wanted him to do probably meant they would reject him or make fun of him, which was difficult for him, because being accepted by everyone was very important to him.

Pleasing all people all the time is an impossible goal. The only realistic goal is to be yourself and choose actions that please God. When your image on the outside matches your image on the inside and you know God approves, you'll be at peace with yourself. You can then be content to be you—the imperfect you—knowing you don't have to earn anyone's approval to feel OK about yourself. If you try to please others, you'll always be wishy-washy and double-minded; there are so many different opinions and so many people to please that you'll be unstable in all areas of your life (James 1:8).

The next time you're in a room of men and women, look around. You'll find people you don't want to get to know because they're different than you. Others you may enjoy talking to but wouldn't want to be good friends or partners with. There are some you might want to be good friends with, but fewer still that you would want to be bosom buddies with and probably very few of the opposite gender you would want to marry.

Does your different level of feeling for each of these people make them any less or more valuable? What do your preferences for people say about them? Nothing! It says only that you prefer a certain type of person to be close to, because you're you and have certain likes and dislikes. Get the point? If someone rejects you as a partner or a friend, does his or her rejection make you unacceptable? Is it a statement about you or about the other person? The other person! It doesn't say anything at all about your actual value or worth.

PROTECTING OTHERS' MASKS

You may find yourself in the difficult position of choosing whether or not to help other people to continue wearing their masks. This most often happens in the context of addictions, personality problems, mental illness, and actions or faults that people want to cover up out of fear of being found out. It's natural to want to protect others from pain, especially when you're close to them. The consequences of discovery may affect the person and you and your family as well. Covering up may feel like the natural thing to do, but it isn't necessarily the right thing to do.

Linda's husband, Randy, was the pastor of a large church. He was respected and loved by the church members and his staff. Other women envied Linda because she was married to such a wonderful man. Linda knew her husband was wearing a mask. He had a secret addiction to pornography that had come to light early in their 15-year marriage. She also knew that Randy loved the Lord, but he refused to admit he needed help. He was often withdrawn, angry, self-absorbed, and blaming. She was hurt and in pain and tired of wearing her mask of the happily married pastor's wife. She struggled with her options. If she told the elders, her husband would be asked to step down, and the church body would suffer. If she separated from him without an explanation and the truth didn't come out, she would be judged for leaving her husband without biblical grounds. If she continued to ignore the problem, he wouldn't get better.

Linda's dilemma was common: continue to cover or expose the mask and cause immediate consequences for many people. While not all people have the additional burden of being the pastor's wife, the circumstances are nonetheless complicated. Scriptural guidelines are clear: Matthew 18:15-17 says we should first go to the person alone in private; then if he or she doesn't listen, take a few others with you, and then if his or her heart continues to be hard, take it a step further and bring the issue out in public. We need to exercise caution and wisdom in bringing other people in to confront, as the people we expose the information to must be chosen carefully. The principle of confronting people who are hardened in their sin is also reinforced in other passages. We're to gently confront those caught in sin but to do so in a way that restores them and doesn't cause shame (Gal. 6:1; 1 Cor. 4:14-16). The apostle Paul instructed the Corinthian believers to forgive and comfort those who had been exposed so that they would not be overcome with sorrow (2 Cor. 2:5-11). We're to expose darkness rather than cover it up (Eph. 5:11), because God established the law of reaping what you sow in order to bring about repentance and change (Gal. 6:7-8). Helping people to keep their masks on prevents them from experiencing the consequences of their actions.

That doesn't mean you go around telling other people's secrets and faults. That isn't the purpose. All of us wear masks, and it's up to the individual to choose what to expose. The only time you can expose someone's mask is when the person is hardened in sin that's damaging him or her and others, and he or she has repeatedly refused to deal with the sin. Even then, your motives must be pure, without pride, and in the best interest of the other person, and your heart has to be cleaned up first (Gal. 6:1).

LIVING IN TRUTH

Taking off your false masks means that you risk being real and willing to live in truth. God searches our hearts and knows what's in them; we aren't hiding anything from Him (Ps. 7:9; Heb. 4:12). God desires truth in our inner parts, which requires honesty first with yourself (Ps. 51:6) and then with others.

QUESTIONS FOR REFLECTION

1. Review the masks in the section "Covering Your Pain." Which of the masks do you wear?

2. Which parts of yourself do you have difficulty expressing: your needs, fears, sadness, jealousy, anger, uncertainty, pain, hurts, joy, spontaneity, weakness, or strengths?

3. Do you use the defensives of denial, blame, rationalization, or justification to cover your feelings of inadequacy and weakness? How do these defensives affect your self-image?

4. How do you try to prove your worthiness to yourself, others, and God? If you didn't have accomplishments and the ability to be productive, would you still know and feel that you're valuable and worthy?

5. How do you protect other people and enable them to continue wearing their masks? How does it benefit and hurt your self-image and the self-images of others?

6. When do you feel arrogant and superior to others? What's really going on inside you when you do this?

7. Are you comfortable being who you are, or do you adjust your image to be what others want you to be? How does this people-pleasing affect your self-image?

8. Look back over the list of "faulty beliefs" in the section "Adjusting Your Image," and identify the ones you hold. Reflect on the corresponding "truths" instead, and write how holding those beliefs would affect your ability to be who you really are, whether or not it pleases other people.

9. What hurts have you experienced that have made it hard for you to trust people and to reveal your true self?

10. Describe when and how you portray a false self. Are there any times and situations when it's easier for you to take off your mask?

7

REAL

images

*WHATEVER IS TRUE, WHATEVER IS
NOBLE, WHATEVER IS RIGHT,
WHATEVER IS PURE, WHATEVER IS
LOVELY, WHATEVER IS ADMIRABLE—
IF ANYTHING IS EXCELLENT OR
PRAISEWORTHY—THINK ABOUT
SUCH THINGS.*
—PHIL. 4:8

7

REAL

images

WHATEVER IS TRUE, WHATEVER IS
NOBLE, WHATEVER IS RIGHT,
WHATEVER IS PURE, WHATEVER IS
LOVELY, WHATEVER IS ADMIRABLE—
IF ANYTHING IS EXCELLENT OR
PRAISEWORTHY—THINK ABOUT
SUCH THINGS.
—PHIL. 4:8

The search for a real image necessitates shattering the myths that come from reflected, projected, damaged, stained, and false images. You're not stuck with the images that society and others have given you or with your limited image of yourself. Discovering your real self-image means finding out who God uniquely created you to be and molding your image to reflect the image of Jesus Christ, His Son. In this way, your self-image will be rooted in truth and reality.

God's desire for each of us is to project a real image that matches our outsides to our insides. It involves vulnerability, transparency, truthfulness, and honesty. It accurately measures who we are. Christ reflected His true image and the image of His Father. He was not afraid to show strength and weakness. Our real image should also reflect the image of Christ.

God gave each of us unique talents that He expects us to use wisely as faithful stewards. Understanding, accepting, enhancing, and enjoying our uniqueness is part of that faithful stewardship. The ability to have a real image results from acceptance of ourselves as we were made and of God's unconditional love toward us.

Since the beginning of time, people have searched for ways to make their lives meaningful and to answer the questions "Who am I?" and "Why am I here?" Finding your real self-image fulfills that search by giving your life meaning, purpose, and satisfaction.

A REAL IMAGE IS ACCURATE

The person with a real self-image sees himself or herself accurately and admits and accepts both the good and the bad.

The apostle Paul tells us in Rom. 12:3, "Do not think of yourself more highly than you ought, but rather think of yourself with sober judgment, in accordance with the measure of faith God has given you." If you see yourself as being good in an area you are not, your assessment is inaccurate. If distortions about yourself prevent you from seeing your abilities, that is also an inaccurate assessment.

Stan was a successful businessman with a thriving company and a nice family. Stan's father had been very critical of him and constantly told him that he wouldn't amount to anything in life. Stan accepted his father's damaged image but also tried to prove him wrong. When he found his niche, he worked diligently and was rewarded with a successful small business. But he continued to see himself as a failure. His self-image wasn't real; it was inaccurate.

Paula dreamed of being a professional dancer. She tried out for various famous ballet companies but wasn't accepted. She continues to see herself as a gifted and talented dancer and blames the evaluators for discriminating against her for no reason. Others can see that she is good but not great. If Paula accurately assesses her talents, she'll be able to accept her limitations. As a result, instead of being bitter and resentful, she can seek to maximize her talents in a way that will bring her success. She could teach ballet to young children or perform locally, both of which she now feels are beneath her abilities.

Identifying and understanding your inborn temperament and natural abilities will help you have a more accurate image of yourself. Clara accepted her inability to be a natural leader like her sister when she understood that her natural temperament was to be an introvert. She began to recognize her own positive aspects, such as her intuitiveness and her ability to think deeply about things.

Taylor needed structure in his life—the exact opposite of his wife, who liked to be spontaneous. When they both understood their differences without judging the other, they were able to accept themselves and each other. Justin was laid back and easy-going, but his brother, Rudy, was intense and driven. Managing their business together was difficult until they realized that their differences balanced each other and made them a perfect team.

Thinking accurately about yourself also involves differentiating between what you were and are. Paul described himself as having been a blasphemer, persecutor, and violent man but stressed that as a result of Christ's grace and love, he was now a faithful servant of the Lord (I Tim. 1:12-14). We, too, were once in darkness but are now children of light (Eph. 5:8). We don't have to be ashamed about what we've done in the past, because we're forgiven. What we used to be and do and now no longer are or do is proof of God's mercy, grace, and patience (1 Tim. 1:15-17).

Susan was promiscuous as a teen and young adult and had an abortion at age 18. She couldn't shake the stained image of herself as a woman who had an abortion. She didn't feel worthy of being happy in her marriage or with her new baby. If Susan's self-image were accurate, she would acknowledge her past mistakes and see herself as she is now—forgiven and free in the Lord. She can hold her head high as a daughter of the King and a faithful servant of the Lord and enjoy what He has given her today.

The past is a part of who we are. God uses everything for His purposes—even our mistakes. We can comfort others with the comfort we have received and with the things we have learned (2 Cor. 1:4). Once Susan is healed and set free from her past, she can reach out to other women who have had abortions or who are considering them. One of the ways we heal and reconcile our stained images is to reach out to others.

A real image results from an accurate and continual self-examination that enables you to admit the truth about your flaws, sins, and strengths (2 Cor. 13:5). It wasn't easy for Dawn to admit that she was frequently impatient with her children. It was easier to see herself as a patient and loving mommy, but she had to admit first that she lost her temper before she could learn to handle difficult situations differently. Unless we face the truth about ourselves and admit our sins, we won't be able to change (1 John 1:8-10).

A REAL IMAGE IS TRANSPARENT

A person with a real image is willing to be transparent. That means that people can see from the outside what's inside. It means you admit your weaknesses, fears, sins, inadequacies, and quirks and show the vulnerable part of you that isn't perfect—the part that questions, doubts, resents, hurts, fears, stumbles, and despairs. Jesus was transparent. We saw His real emotions: anger (Mark 11:15-17), irritation (Matt. 15:16), sadness (John 11:35), joy (John 15:11), love (John 15:12-13), disappointment (Matt. 26:40), and deep inner turmoil (Matt. 26:38-39). Paul was also transparent about his emotions and struggles (2 Cor. 4:8) and his sins, temptations, and weaknesses (Rom. 7:19-24). King David regularly invites us to see his emotional and personal struggles throughout the Psalms.

Each of us plays various roles, such as those of wife, husband, father, daughter, son, employee, friend, volunteer, or athlete. These roles are a big part of your image. Each defines you, and each limits you. For example, as a husband or wife, you see yourself as a committed partner rather than a single person looking to date. Your parental role shapes your image into one of being a responsible and sacrificial adult. Your employee role describes you too. Regardless of what kind of work you do, your job title describes a part of you and probably is no accident, because you chose it. Something about it fits you. Roles become part of your self-image, but they're not all of you. It can be easy to lose yourself behind your roles and refuse to let people see you as you really are. There's a part of you that's more *you* than these roles: The real you that has inadequacies, fears, hurts, desires, joys, and dreams.

You may be afraid that you'll be judged, rejected, or ridiculed, especially if you've experienced those things in past relationships. Some persons put on a false image that portrays them as always strong, in control, righteous, wise, fearless, and capable because they fear revealing the truth about their inadequacies. Others put on an image of weakness, inability, and dependency due to fear of taking risks. False images block transparency and keep us from receiving encouragement, support, and love. But it's worth taking the risk, because the payoff will eventually be good.

Sharing our faults with others helps us let go of the shame and aids our healing (James 5:16). Why is that? When we openly admit our faults, we're being real and are facing the fear that we're worse than others and unacceptable to God and others. Finding out that we're only human and that others understand, accept us, and identify with our struggles helps us feel less isolated and flawed. Keeping secrets increases the powerful hold they have on our lives; admitting our secrets sets us free. One of the reasons recovery support groups are so effective is that they allow people to admit the truth about themselves among others who have done the same thing. These groups offer unconditional acceptance and hope for future change.

Discretion is necessary, not only in what we share but also in who we share with. Choose someone who is gracious and humble and won't use your admission against you. It isn't appropriate to tell your boss and coworkers everything about your past, your personal life, and your marital problems. But it may be appropriate to share those things with one or two of your coworkers who can support you or identify with you. You may want to share your inner struggles with a few friends who are trustworthy—but not necessarily with the whole church. Some family members are safe and supportive, and others aren't. Don't share vulnerabilities with people who will use them against you or tell others.

When you're vulnerable, others will be too. In counseling, I encounter people who are in deep emotional pain. They're often in church groups but haven't shared any of their trials with anyone. They're under the false impression that they're the only ones struggling. I sometimes suggest that they risk sharing some of their pain in the group or at least with one person. To their surprise, when they do, others often begin sharing their pain too. Being willing to share our struggles often makes it safe for others to share theirs. In this way, we bear each other's burdens (Gal. 6:2).

Unfortunately, there are times when others aren't willing to share their struggles but are invested heavily in maintaining the false image that they don't have problems or weaknesses (1 John 1:8). In this case, your disclosure may be met with judgment rather than encouragement and understanding. If this happens to you, continue to look for safe people to be open with.

Heather was in deep emotional pain. She had a troubled marriage along with a son who was heavily into drugs. Everyone else seemed to be so perfect that after Bible study she felt even worse about her life than before. She could hardly stand the shame she felt when comparing her life to theirs. One day one of the other ladies who appeared to have it all together started to cry. She admitted that her husband had left her for another woman and that she was barely able to function. The women rallied around her, and two ladies admitted that their husbands had prior affairs. One had stayed with her husband, and the other had divorced. Heather was finally free to share her pain, and when she did, she found other women who had children with addictions and similar marital problems.

Sarah's sister-in-law Angie always seemed distant to her. They never talked about serious things, and Angie never admitted having any problems. Sarah knew things weren't good, because Angie's husband was out of work and drank too much. One day Angie broke down and shared her struggles. Sarah instantly felt a kinship with her that she hadn't experienced before. Sharing your vulnerabilities and being transparent allows people to respond to the real you. You'll not only find that you feel more loved and accepted, but you'll feel closer too. Intimacy flourishes with transparency and vulnerability.

A REAL IMAGE IS UNIQUE

Before you were even formed, God knew you (Jer. 1:5). You are "fearfully and wonderfully made" by God, who put you together in your mother's womb (Ps. 139:13-14). God likens himself to a potter who forms clay pots on the wheel according to His own purpose and design. The pot cannot say to the potter, "Why did you make me this way?" because the potter has the right to do what He wishes with His creation (Isa. 29:16; Rom. 9:20).

Accepting ourselves as God made us can be one of the most difficult parts of discovering a real image. God wants us to accept ourselves as His unique creation and rejoice in it. When you wish you were someone else, you aren't able to be who you are. When I write, I have to write according to my abilities. I occasionally find myself reading someone else's writing and comparing it to my own, thinking, *What am I doing? I can't write compared to this person.* When I compare myself to others, I want to quit writing. Yet I have something they don't: me. That's what enables me to write *my* book. And that's what enables you to live *your* life. In order to find your real image, you must let go of the reflected images from society and other people and stop trying to be someone else.

God created you to be uniquely you and has a plan for your unique abilities. Not accepting yourself as you are prevents you from fulfilling His purpose for you.

Each of us has been given gifts or talents, and we're responsible for using those talents (Matt. 25:14-30). If you're not sure what your gifts and talents are, pay attention to the opportunities that come your way. Watch to see what motivates and energizes you. Passion breeds excitement and enthusiasm. As you step out and try various things, you'll discover what God created you to do. If fear of being yourself holds you back from investing your talents, you'll waste what God has given you (Matt. 25:24-30).

The man in the parable of the talents gave his servants varying amounts of money and responsibility according to their individual ability (Matt. 25:15). God has done the same with us. We each have different gifts and functions within the Church body and our lives (Rom. 12:5-6; Eph. 4:11; 1 Cor. 12:4-11, 28). In our humanness, we judge what God has given us as important or unimportant, big or small, special or ordinary, spiritual or worldly, good or bad. In God's eyes, these divisions don't exist. In fact, God's system is the opposite of ours. He uses the lowly things and the things that are despised by the world rather than the things that the world admires

(1 Cor. 1:26-28) and values the weaker parts more than the more prominent parts (1 Cor. 12:24-25). God will use the very things you hate about yourself to bring glory to Him and to cause you to depend on Him (2 Cor. 12:7-10). Nothing is wasted with God. All your experiences, trials, hardships, and even failures are parts of you that God will use for your good, the good of others, and His glory (Gen. 50:20; Rom. 8:28).

Mavis felt disappointment because of the choices she had made: getting pregnant in her teens, marrying the baby's father, then divorcing and marrying another man who wasn't a Christian. When she focused on her mistakes, she felt defeated, but when she reached out and used her experiences to help others, she felt redeemed. Jay was ashamed to admit that he had spent time in prison for robbery, but out of that came a heart to work with troubled youth in his church and community. Both Jay and Mavis began to see their pasts as experiences that could be used for God.

We'll all give an account of our faithfulness with the gifts, talents, and opportunities God has given us (1 Cor. 4:2). God's system of judging faithfulness is completely fair, because it's not dependent on the type of talent or the results. God gives different gifts but expects the same faithfulness from all. He'll judge your efforts, not the outcome of those efforts. The outcome is His responsibility (1 Cor. 3:5-9).

A REAL IMAGE IS HONEST

God is a God of truth. He wants us to have truth on the inside and the outside (Ps. 51:6). He hates lies, pretense, and deceitfulness (Prov. 6:17-19). Honesty is absolutely necessary to please Him. Christians often have difficulty differentiating between honesty and pride. You will often hear them saying things like "God gets all the glory—I didn't do anything" or "It's not about me." Pastor Wilson shared that his ministry has really prospered. "One thousand people have joined my church in the last two years," he explained, "but not because of anything I've done."

I don't think God is displeased with comments that describe your efforts and abilities. It isn't wrong to admit the truth about what you do and who you are or to feel good about yourself! There's a direct link between your actions and the outcome. My husband has worked very hard to build a construction pipeline business. Yes, we look at the business and see how God has blessed it, but my husband gets a lot of the credit. It was his effort to get up very early in the morning, day after day, and work late into the night and on weekends. Without his diligence, God wouldn't have blessed a business that never was, and it wouldn't be providing for our family.

How silly we must sound at times to the world! To pretend that you don't get any credit or that you can't truthfully state what you do or are good at is false humility. Stating the truth in the right spirit is true humility.

We don't have to pretend we're worthless to please God. He values His creation, and we're part of that creation. He knows the talents He gave us and delights in their use. And He will compliment you for a job well done when you see Him (Matt. 25:23).

Yet there's a balance that must be carefully maintained when you admit what you do well. Responding to a compliment with "Yeah, I know I'm good" would display a lack of social skill and arrogance. If you accept a compliment graciously, you're not being prideful. I asked my sixth-grade daughter, Lindsey, whether it's OK to feel good about getting an award. She said, "Getting an award is good. Feeling good about it is OK unless you think too much about it and brag—then you're proud, and that's bad." Then she added, "I don't like to be around people who brag, because they're always putting you down and trying to be better than everyone else."

If you praise yourself too much and begin to think you're special, good, or superior to others, you have become proud. Be careful when assuming you're wise or gifted, because you can always be knocked off your pedestal by someone better than you (Prov. 25:6-7). It might be better to wait for someone else to praise you (Prov. 27:2).

Boasting seeks to promote or display oneself in a way that invites praise. It exults in one's own ability, exaggerating the goodness, displaying it in a way that shows you desire to be the center of attention and superior to others. It says, "Look at me—I'm the best." True humility, in contrast, states the truth without comparing oneself to others, so there's no opportunity to feel prideful. How you say it matters too. A simple statement of "I'm a good teacher" can be said with or without sinful pride, depending on your attitude, body language, tone, and relationship with the person you're speaking to.

You are ultimately to strive to please God above everyone else. If you're insecure about yourself and dependent on the compliments or opinions of others, you'll tend to make choices with the goal of pleasing others to receive praise from them. Or you'll take an absence of compliments to prove you've failed when that may not be the case. All of us desire affirmation, so getting compliments from others is appreciated, but it shouldn't be our main goal. Pleasing God is what matters most (Gal. 1:10).

A REAL IMAGE IS HUMBLE

Humility is a truthful and realistic view of yourself—the opposite of conceit (Rom. 12:3). Humility means you're able to assess and admit your strengths and weaknesses. Paul says that he would "not boast beyond proper limits, but will confine [his] boasting to the field God has assigned to [him]" (2 Cor. 10:13). He was contrasting himself with the false teachers who were taking credit for things they didn't do (2 Cor. 10:12).

God gives us life, gifts, talents, and the opportunity to succeed to begin with (Deut. 8:17-18 & 1 Cor. 4:7). When we keep this in mind, we will not become proud. We will feel a humble gratitude rather than pride, knowing that it is by God's grace and goodness that we have what we have and are what we are.

The apostle Paul could have boasted, but he didn't want to use his achievements to gain influence with the believers. Instead, he focused on the fact that his competence came from the Lord and that it was God who called and equipped him to be a minister (2 Cor. 3:4-6). On his own, he was killing Christians rather than converting them to the faith. Paul didn't take credit for his calling but admitted that he was being diligent to follow it. We can recognize our abilities and our efforts but not delude ourselves into thinking they're a way of gaining favor with God, salvation, or righteousness or that they make us any better than anyone else (Phil. 3:3-9).

A proud person has something at stake—he or she needs to be good. Not being good is either not possible or unacceptable. This characteristic is related to a complete dependence on self and what other people think and is the result of a low self-image. Paul said this about Diotrephes, stating that he "loves to be first," so he refused to cooperate with other Christians and gossiped about them maliciously

(3 John 9-10), acting destructively toward others out of his wounded egotistical pride. A person who has to be good will not be able to co-operate with others, allow others to be more talented, admit wrong, accept failure, or follow advice—all the characteristics of a fool.

People who continually talk about how lowly they are may actually be self-centered, because the focus is still on self. Not only will they not be able to freely give to others, but because they think they aren't worthy, they won't be able to take their minds off them-selves to think about others. Truly humble people are not self-ab-sorbed, because they're at peace with themselves, know who they are, and can freely give. It's as if they're "over themselves" and able to be "other-focused."

John the Baptist understood this truth. He knew he was to use his talents to draw attention to the coming of Jesus. He faithfully did what he was called to do but knew Jesus was the main act (John 3:27-30). Jesus understood it, too, and lived to do the will of His Fa-ther (John 6:38). The apostle Paul knew it when he said that he lived for Christ, not for himself (Phil. 1:21). All these people knew who they were and were able to accept themselves completely and then get on with life.

A person with a real self-image can receive criticism, but a proud and foolish person can't (Prov. 12:15). A proud person has an unrealistically inflated self-image and is unwilling to acknowl-edge personal flaws. Many people have difficulty responding open-ly and positively to criticism, because they equate disapproval with a loss of love. When you're offered reproof, exhortation, or sugges-tions, you may actually be the recipient of an act motivated by love —the kind of love that has your best interest in mind and wants to see the best in you (Gal. 6:1; Rom. 13:10).

Tyson didn't want to hear that his anger was harming his family. He angrily accused his wife of trying to control him and make him look bad. He refused to look at himself. Carol struggled with hearing what her friend had to say about her attitude. Her initial response was to defend herself, but she swallowed her pride and instead listened to her concerns and analyzed her recent actions and motives. In the end, she could see that she had pulled away from her best friend to be more accepted by the new girl at the office.

A REAL IMAGE IS WORTHY

If you're a person with a real image, you know you're worthy and valuable—because God says so. God knows what you're made of yet loves and accepts you (Ps. 103:14). Your worth isn't related to what you do, who you are, what you have, or what you look like. It comes from being God's creation. God valued you enough to send His Son to purchase you, so don't become a slave to the value system of people, which diminishes your worth (1 Cor. 7:23).

When you know you're worthy in God's eyes just as you are, you don't have to work to be accepted or to prove yourself. God offers unconditional love that you can't lose (Rom. 8:35-39).

A woman near my home was attacked a few years ago by a mountain lion and left with significant scars on her face. Amazingly, she readily dismissed the disfigurement. She gave testimony to her faith in God, said she trusted Him completely, and didn't depend on her looks at all. She appeared not to notice the change. I want that kind of self-image, one that looks inward and upward rather than outward.

Acceptance of who you are today frees you to live your life fully. Poor self-worth originates from self-pity. When you conclude that you're lowly and worthless and that nothing in you is good, you surrender to a lie. God doesn't want you to believe you're useless and lowly, because it isn't true.

A REAL IMAGE IMITATES CHRIST

God created people in His own image (Gen. 1:26-27). That likeness was marred when Adam and Eve sinned. God restored our images through the death of Jesus Christ. Jesus is "the image of the invisible God" (Col. 1:15) and "the head of the body, the church" (Col. 1:18). "For God was pleased to have all his fullness dwell in him, and through him to reconcile to himself all things, . . . through his blood, shed on the cross. Once you were alienated from God and were enemies in your minds because of your evil behavior. But now he has reconciled you by Christ's physical body through death to present you holy in his sight, without blemish and free from accusation" (Col. 1:19-22).

When God looks at you, He sees His Son's image unblemished and righteous. When you look at yourself, do you see His image or your own? Do you see yourself as the child of the King, redeemed, loved, accepted, and holy? It changes your image when you can see yourself as His redeemed child.

Jesus Christ didn't have outer beauty that impressed people (Isa. 53:2), but He did make an impression with His character. You received a new nature when you were saved, which allows you to choose not to live by the old sinful nature (Gal. 5:16) but instead to live in a way that imitates Christ.

You're also part of Christ's body, the Church. Do you see yourself as part of the Body of Christ or alone in your Christian walk? This Body is made up of many parts, each one with its own role or function. All are important and necessary, no matter how small (1 Cor. 12:12-27). The Church is the representation of God to the world (Eph. 3:10-11). Seeing yourself as a part of that Body changes your image. It makes your purpose and your existence bigger than you and significant, no matter how trivial you think your life is. You're a part of God's purpose and plan in this world and throughout eternity. He has a specific purpose for you that He'll fulfill in you (Ps. 138:8). Enlarge your vision of who you are to fit God's view of you. You matter!

Your real image includes Christ's image. People need to see Jesus through you by your actions and your love. Moses spent time with God on Mount Sinai. When he came down, his face was radiant, but he didn't even know it (Exod. 34:29). You can have that essence or radiance of Jesus in your life through your relationship with Him.

QUESTIONS FOR REFLECTION

1. How does your image of yourself compare with who you really are?

2. Are you able to be transparent and real with other people? Which things about you are you most afraid to reveal?

3. Think of some situations in which you were transparent and real. What reactions did people have? How did your transparency affect the relationship? Did these experiences encourage you or discourage you from being real in the future?

4. Which things about you do you have difficulty accepting? How do you think God wants you to view those things?

5. What roles do you play in your life? How are those roles part of your self-image? Do any of them help you hide the real you?

6. List some of your unique talents and gifts. Do you use them, or does your lack of confidence prevent you from developing them and becoming all God wants for you?

7. Can you feel good about what you do without feeling that you're sinning? Can you genuinely accept compliments, or do you believe it's wrong for you to say anything good about yourself? Name some things about yourself that you feel good about.

8. How are you self-focused, other-focused, and God-focused? How does low self-worth and low self-esteem keep you self-focused and prevent you from truly being God-focused and other-focused in healthful ways?

9. Picture yourself in God's eyes. How does He see you? Do you feel worthy, loved, and accepted—or unworthy, criticized, punished, or ashamed?

10. Do you see yourself as an important part of the Body of Christ, or do you see yourself as unimportant and unnecessary? What part of the Body are you? How does seeing yourself as an important part of the Body change your self-image?

8

MAINTAINING YOUR REAL

image

*DO NOT CONFORM ANY LONGER TO
THE PATTERN OF THIS WORLD,
BUT BE TRANSFORMED BY THE
RENEWING OF YOUR MIND. THEN YOU
WILL BE ABLE TO TEST AND APPROVE
WHAT GOD'S WILL IS—HIS GOOD,
PLEASING AND PERFECT WILL.*
—ROM. 12:2

8

MAINTAINING YOUR REAL

image

DO NOT CONFORM ANY LONGER TO
THE PATTERN OF THIS WORLD,
BUT BE TRANSFORMED BY THE
RENEWING OF YOUR MIND. THEN YOU
WILL BE ABLE TO TEST AND APPROVE
WHAT GOD'S WILL IS—HIS GOOD,
PLEASING AND PERFECT WILL.

—ROM. 12:2

A real image requires maintenance. If you begin again to compare yourself to the standards of others, your real image will suffer. Your relationships will continue to provide you with interactions that can damage your self-image. It's important to remain diligent to reject the damaged images, projected images, reflected images, stained images, and false images that we're all prone to. You'll have to continue to risk being vulnerable and transparent rather than defensive and closed.

CONTROL YOUR THOUGHTS

The most important thing you can do to maintain your real image is to control your thoughts. You are what you think you are (Prov. 23:7, KJV), so your self-image is what you think it is. You can take your thoughts captive and make them obedient to Christ by countering false statements that lead you to have an inaccurate self-image (2 Cor. 10:5). Your thoughts affect your perceptions and your feelings, which in turn affect your attitudes and actions. It isn't the circumstances in your life that create your reality, but what you think or believe about them (Rom. 12:2). If you change your thoughts about yourself, you'll feel differently about yourself.

Contrast these thoughts: "I'm ugly—no one will ever love me" with "I'm valuable and worthy of being loved." "I'm too stupid to do this right" with "I can do the best I can, and that's OK." "I'm inept" with "That was hard for me, but there are other things I do well." You can easily see how these thoughts could shape your self-image and result in entirely different feelings, attitudes, and actions.

You're thinking all the time. And part of the time your thoughts are talking to you. This "self-talk" can work positively or negatively. I challenge you to listen to your self-talk. It will probably surprise you and give you some insight into what you believe about yourself and how your thoughts affect your self-image and your life.

Some of your self-talk is a recording of the damaged images and messages from your past. If one or both of your parents were shaming or critical of you, your self-talk will contain shaming and critical messages. If you listen, you'll hear that parent's message re-played in your head. Other people's voices are also a part of your self-talk. If someone put you down and you accepted that damaged image as your own, you will have integrated that message into your self-talk. Once you identify the damaged messages, you must active-ly listen for them and counter them with truth until they go away.

Sal's dad ridiculed him for not being masculine enough. He called him a "sissy," a "momma's boy," a "girl," and a "wimp." Sal wasn't allowed to cry without being scolded, and he was always shamed for not being tough or for running to his mother. As an adult, Sal doesn't feel adequate and is constantly trying to prove he is masculine. When he's emotional, he hears a voice saying, "You're a sissy. Toughen up." When he feels afraid, he calls himself a "girl." When he admits to himself that he needs his wife or gives in to her requests, he tells himself that he's a pushover and a wimp. Sal's self-image is distorted by the damaged images from the past. He first needs to recognize those messages, see how they're affecting him today, challenge them to see if they're true, and then adjust his thinking. He must realize that his dad's image of the ideal child and man were distorted.

Megan's mom was an alcoholic. She didn't take good care of Megan or her little sister. She was also critical, controlling, and ma-nipulative. Megan heard these messages from her mom: "Do a bet-ter job." "It's selfish for you to leave your little sister alone today." "I need you, so you can't go out." Megan continues to struggle with conflicted feelings about her childhood and her mother. On one hand, she's angry with her mother, but when she thinks anything bad about her mother, she tells herself, *You're so ungrateful. Mom wasn't so bad.* When she takes care of herself or says no to people, she hears, "You're so selfish. You don't care about anyone but yourself." Megan's mother's messages have become part of her self-talk that says she needs to change. But it isn't a betrayal to face the truth about your parents. It's OK to put your needs first, and you don't always have to take care of other people.

Self-talk is usually shame-talk. Shame-talk is that inner voice that beats you up, puts you down, and tells you that you're bad, not good enough, less than, and unworthy. It compares you to others and concludes you don't measure up. Shame-talk often originates from difficult relationships and childhood. It reaches into the past and pulls out stained, projected, and damaged images that consist of accusations, labels, mistakes, and projections and adds them to the present failures. Shame-talk has to be identified, because it's toxic. It poisons your self-image and keeps you from changing, because it tells you that you aren't any good.

The antidote to shame-talk is to replace it with forgiveness, truth, and acceptance. If it's a stained image, you did the best you could. God has forgiven you, so you can forgive yourself, let go of the need to beat yourself up, and move on. You did what you did at the time because of who you were and the circumstances you were in. If you had had the tools to do it differently, you would have. Accept that, and let it go. If it's a damaged or projected image, replace it with truth.

You aren't stuck with your negative self-talk. Low self-esteem doesn't prove you aren't worthy. It's the result of judgments and experiences that have damaged your self-image. You can choose to change those images and see yourself as you really are: loved by God, worthy of being loved, and valuable regardless of whether other people love or have loved you and affirmed your worth.

LET GO OF PLEASING OTHERS

All of us prefer to be approved by others. Even God loves to be praised, and we are created in His image with His attributes. Approval is nice, but when the approval of others dictates who you are, you're on shaky ground, and your real self-image is under attack. Once you've identified and established your personal convictions, ideas, and perceptions and have discovered your real image, it will be easier to let go of the need to please people.

You can listen to the opinions and counsel of other people, but you must be aware of the fact that their opinions and perceptions may be inaccurate. What they think about you is filtered through their own experiences, preconceived ideas, emotions, prejudices, and personal agendas. You can't please everyone, so it's best to just focus on being yourself.

Be aware of your need to please. Listen to the warning thoughts that you may be a people-pleaser, such as *What does he [she] think of me? Does he [she] like me? I don't want him [her] to be angry. He [She] is better than me.* When you hear thoughts like these, refocus your attention and remind yourself that getting that person's positive opinion, approval, or affection is worth it only if it's because you're being the real you. If you have to change yourself to get it, you're deluding yourself. Approval for a false image you're putting forth isn't really approval of you but is approval of a *false* you! Remember—you can survive disapproval, even though it might be unpleasant.

Part of discovering your real self-image involves identifying who you are—including what you believe, value, think, want, and need. Part of maintaining your image involves being able to stand firm even when others disagree with you.

Adults aren't exempt from peer pressure. John the Baptist was able to be totally different. His clothes were made from camel's hair, and his food was primarily locusts and wild honey (Matt. 3:4). Most of us can't go that far. We dress fashionably, change our hair-style to fit the trend, and talk like the people we're around. Other pressures include the choices we make, the activities we take part in, the things we laugh at, and the beliefs we hold.

Is your self-image strong enough to "just say no" to the things you know are wrong for you? Or do you need to fit in so badly that you allow yourself to be swayed? (1 Cor. 15:33). Do you go to or rent questionable movies, look at pornography, laugh at dirty jokes, keep your faith and opinions a secret, and refuse to stand up for what you know is right because you're afraid of disap-proval? If so, you're not living true to your real image. Monitor the effects of society's norms and adult peer pressure on your choices, and make a stand that fits your real image so you'll be congruent on the inside and outside.

HOLD REALISTIC EXPECTATIONS

If your expectations are reasonable and realistic, they work in your favor by propelling you toward workable goals. But when they're unreasonable and unrealistic, you'll find yourself frustrated, unhappy, and enslaved. Unrealistic expectations are like the law.

They drag you back into a rigid standard that keeps you from enjoying your freedom (Gal. 5:1-4) and can't make you perfect anyway (Heb. 7:18-19).

It's best to avoid all extremes (Eccles. 7:15-18). Perfectionism is an extreme. Accept it now: You're not perfect, and you're not going to be perfect. Yes, you can always do better, but you can't be good enough to *earn* God's love. You'll always be able to say, as Paul did, "Not that I have already obtained all this, or have already been made perfect," but I keep pressing on, "forgetting what is behind and straining toward what is ahead" (Phil. 3:12-13).

Expectations often come in the form of "shoulds." Expectations cause you to say things like "I should sacrifice more." "I should do better." "I should make more money." "I should do something important." "I should be happy." "I should be satisfied." "I shouldn't be angry or hurt." "I should be skinnier." "I should visit my family." "I should like my job." When you do this, you're comparing yourself to an internal ideal that often brings shame and guilt with it. The shame makes you feel badly for being who you are and as a result often keeps you stuck in a negative, self-defeating cycle rather than motivating you to do better.

"Shoulds" put you into bondage—and you aren't under bondage. Christ set you free from the law and all the "have tos" (1 Cor. 6:12). The apostle Paul also got caught by "shoulds." He wanted to do what he thought was good and right but found that he couldn't always do it. Fortunately, he was able to override that shame-talk with forgiveness talk that said, "There is now no condemnation for those who are in Christ Jesus, because through Christ Jesus the law of the Spirit of life set me free from the law of sin and death" (Rom. 8:1-2).

Keep your expectations about your looks reasonable. There are certain things you cannot change, such as your age, body build, and physical characteristics. Accept them. Maximize what you can, and then quit comparing yourself to others and focusing on the things you don't like! If you're overweight, set reasonable goals, not impossible goals. A loss of 10 pounds is more realistic in the short term than the loss of 100 pounds. As you set your goals, remember that real women aren't the ones we see in magazines and on television; they're in grocery stores, car pools, PTA meetings, in sweats and slippers cleaning their houses and wearing sizes 12 to 14, which are average sizes. Real men aren't the Hollywood stars but the truck drivers, Little League coaches, construction workers, and dads at Home Depot on Saturdays in old jeans and tennis shoes.

Expectations about being a perfect parent are also unreasonable. When you read child-rearing books, you're presented with someone's ideal model. When you embrace the model and don't make room for the fact that you're an imperfect parent raised by imperfect parents and raising imperfect kids, you'll feel as if you fall short. All parents lose it once in a while and react in ways they later regret. Give yourself grace, admit your faults, and move on. You aren't responsible for everything your kids do either. Their successes and failures aren't necessarily a reflection on you or your parenting. They're free to make their own bad or good choices and some make bad ones in spite of the fact that their parents were pretty good parents.

You aren't going to be a perfect Christian, wife, friend, sister, husband, brother, daughter, son, or employee either. Let go of your rigid ideals.

EXAMINE YOURSELF

Maintaining an accurate self-image requires examination through introspection. To do this, you must step outside yourself and observe yourself almost as if you're seeing someone else. This allows you to be impartial and nondefensive. Evaluate your thoughts, attitudes, emotions, and motives. Remember—the purpose of judging yourself isn't to condemn but to assess what needs to change.

When you discover mistakes, don't beat yourself up. Accept your weaknesses, and then try to do better. Many times we're less forgiving of ourselves than we are others. Jane was known as an understanding and compassionate woman, and people found her very encouraging. Yet Jane was harsh toward herself. She frequently berated herself silently and expected more of herself than she did others. She was finally able to quiet the shaming voice in her head by speaking to herself as if she were one of those people who came to her. She said, "It feels so much better to offer myself grace than condemnation. I've even been able to imagine Jesus speaking His grace to me too."

Another way to extend grace toward yourself is to consider the context and use reason. God offers to converse with us regarding our sins (Isa. 1:18). When you're tired, under extra stress, and pulled in several directions at once, your resistance will be down, and you'll probably react differently than when you're feeling better. Remember that it takes time to change your behavior. There may be a time when you become aware of something in your character that needs to be changed but you feel powerless to change it. In time, you'll get the ability to overcome. Keep trying, even if you fail.

Be willing to speak the truth about yourself. Give yourself credit for good things, and praise God for the unique abilities and talents you have. Stop putting yourself down, and instead maintain an accurate, humble, and honest appraisal of yourself.

PROTECT YOUR IMAGE

You'll continue to experience attacks on your real image in the form of projections and damaging messages. You can build a defense against these projections to protect your real image and not let undeserved criticisms (Prov. 26:2), personal differences (Rom. 14:1-4), abuse (1 Pet. 4:4), manipulations (Prov. 26:26), and false accusations (Ps. 35:20) affect your self-image.

Others will put their expectations and demands on you, but that doesn't mean you have to accept them. If you seek to do everything others want you to do, you'll lose yourself.

Not everything people say to you is true. Consider the source. Do they have your best interests in mind? Are they emotionally healthy? Do they know you? What's your history with them? Are they credible? Are they capable of being objective? Are they blaming you for their stuff? Is it someone you love but who's also angry, dysfunctional, controlling, self-centered, hurtful, and manipulative? Remember—just because someone says it doesn't make it so. People say lots of things that aren't true. Guard your heart, because your heart is the center of who you are (Prov. 4:23). If you let your heart be shaped and changed by everything said to you, your real image will be damaged.

There are many kinds of projections you must guard against. If your children want their way, they'll tell you that you're a bad parent. If your boss is stressed, he or she may be more critical of your work. If your spouse goes through periods of emotional instability and is angry during these times, you shouldn't take the things he or she says seriously. If someone is needy and demanding and you rightfully say no to a request, you can expect displeasure, guilt, and pressure. If someone is moody, you don't have to accept responsibility for his or her moods. Emotionally wounded, unstable, dysfunctional, immature, irresponsible, and addicted people blame you for their own problems and emotions. If you pick up their projections, you'll have an inaccurate self-image.

If you're in an abusive relationship, you'll find yourself questioning yourself frequently. You may find yourself confused and rehashing interactions in your mind, trying to figure it all out. You'll doubt your perceptions, question your part, accept blame, feel off-balanced, experience emotional pain, and even wonder if you're crazy.

Mindy is confused. She tries to be a good wife to her husband, Matt, but he's always unhappy with her. He accuses her of trying to undermine him when she offers her opinion. When she does what he asks, he doesn't notice it but finds something else to criticize. When she shares something she's proud of, he ridicules her and minimizes it. When she complains about something that bothers her or asks for something she needs, her husband accuses her of being a selfish nag and tells her she needs to quietly submit. Mindy thinks her motives are right, but it seems that Matt always takes her intentions wrong. She struggles with whether or not to accept his perception of her as a nagging, unloving, and selfish wife since it differs radically from her perception of herself. Mindy is in an emotionally and verbally abusive relationship.

It can be difficult to sort out the projections, manipulations, power plays, and guilt that an abusive person uses, but you must do it if you're to maintain a real self-image. If people close to you who are supposed to love and care about you mistreat you, it can be especially difficult to question their motives and reject their projections. You may need a professional counselor to help you figure it out.

When people judge you by their standards that are different from yours, don't automatically assume they're right and you're wrong. Cassie's husband is a neat freak. She isn't. She can see herself as a failure as a wife because her husband is unhappy with her, or she can realize they have different ideas of what's "neat." If others are unhappy with you, you don't have to judge yourself as wrong. You can accept your right to be who you are and then decide if you want to adapt yourself to them. There are some reasonable accommodations that we need to make in many areas of our lives to live peaceably with other people and to show them that we're cooperating and caring, but that doesn't mean we tell ourselves that we're wrong and they're right, or that we lose our "selves" in the process (Rom. 14:13-21).

Difficult people are adept at using words to avoid taking responsibility for their inaction. One of the ways they do this is to say they want something but do nothing about it. They then use their self-proclaimed intention as a way to prove they did want it, then project blame onto you for the failure, because you didn't recognize or cooperate with their good intention.

Nancy tried really hard to save her marriage, but Lee wouldn't cooperate. He wouldn't admit he was wrong, go to counseling, listen to Nancy's complaints, discuss problems, or admit he had a drug problem. Yet he still stated he didn't want a divorce and was willing to work on the marriage. He accused Nancy of not accepting his efforts and being difficult to please. Nancy ended up questioning herself. Lee effectively shifted the responsibility to Nancy by using words to confuse her. He didn't do anything constructive or tangible to work on the marriage, and Nancy was duped into accepting his words over his action.

When someone's *actions* don't match his or her *words*, be very cautious. It's easy for someone to say he or she is trying to get a job, but are interviews scheduled? Anyone can say he or she is trying to change, but what steps toward change are being taken? When someone claims to be doing something but never seems to be actually doing it, a further manipulation is to shift the responsibility of not recognizing it onto you.

People won't be happy with you when you refuse to bail them out. "You're cold-hearted and mean—you never were a good mom and still aren't!" Jason shouts at his mother, Betty, who just refused to give him money to pay his rent. If Betty believes she's a bad mom because Jason says she is, she'll have an inaccurate image of herself. Immature and self-centered people are pleased with you only when you give them their way. If you need their approval, you'll have to stop doing what's right for you.

Don't assume the responsibility of making other people happy. You aren't responsible for their moods or their choices. If you see yourself as adequate only when other people are feeling good about themselves or you, your self-image will be on a roller-coaster ride.

PURSUE YOUR PASSIONS

Finding your real image involves discovering who God created you to be. Develop confidence and competence. Risk trying different things, and continue to discover your passions and stay true to them. No matter how little time you have, do something that makes you feel alive, motivated, and excited. When you find a passion, it invigorates you. Your real image says, "This is it! This is what I was created for!"

Realistically, though, life may interfere. Getting an education, changing careers, or volunteering your time might be difficult if you're working full-time and raising a family or constrained by other realities. Sadie decided she wanted to be a counselor even though she was 45 years old. She went back to school part-time for six years and graduated at 51. She said, "It was absolutely worth it. I have a new passion for life and am excited about what God will do." Is that where you are today? Don't be discouraged and in despair. Look to the future. There may be something small you can do today. Pursue your goals a little at a time, even if it feels as if they're a long way off.

BEWARE OF COMPARING

Do you compare yourself to others and think everyone is better than you? Do you compare yourself to others and feel *you're* better? Both are wrong comparisons. Instead, "each one should test his own actions. Then he can take pride in himself, without comparing himself to somebody else" (Gal. 6:4). When you stand before God to give an account of your life, you won't be judged on whether you did better or worse than someone else but for what you did with what you had (Matt. 25:14-30).

When you find yourself comparing yourself to someone else, stop. Get your eyes off the other person, and look at yourself. It's never an accurate measurement to look at others. Laura found this truth to be truly liberating. She had always felt like a failure. She wasn't as good in school as her sister, nor was she as pretty. It seemed as if she was always competing with Ann in her mind and heart and never won. After applying this truth, Laura began to compare her current progress to her past progress. She lost five pounds and felt great. "Before, no matter how much I lost, it wasn't enough, because my sister was always thinner. Now I'm happy about losing any weight, because I'm improving myself. I also went back to school to pursue a two-year nursing degree. Ann is a doctor, so becoming a nurse wasn't good enough before, but now it is. A nursing degree is an improvement over what I'm doing now," she says. When you compare your past self to your current self, you can achieve success. It's a winning scenario.

When we compare ourselves to Christ, we'll always fall short. But as we seek to grow in holiness, God helps us to become more and more like Him in attitude, action, and devotion.

ACCEPT YOURSELF AS YOU ARE TODAY

What does it mean to accept yourself as you are? Just that. In this moment, in this time, and in this place, you accept what and who you are. God loves you and offers His unconditional love and acceptance toward you right now (Rom. 15:7). Offer it to yourself too.

Acceptance means that you stop resisting, fighting, denying, challenging, and struggling with who God created you to be. You surrender to the things about yourself that you can't change, including your past, your strengths, your limitations, your inborn personality, and your physical appearance. You accept your humanness and inability to be perfect. Paradoxically, offering yourself acceptance allows you to grow and change the things you can, while nonacceptance keeps you stuck.

Acceptance of yourself allows you to be real with others. When you're transparent with people, they'll feel free to be open with you. Your vulnerability will help them feel accepted by you (Rom. 15:7). Your ability to offer grace to yourself will be a powerful testimony of God's grace toward them.

And remember—your real image will change as you grow in understanding, knowledge, and maturity in the Lord. God isn't through with you yet. You're a work in progress!

QUESTIONS FOR REFLECTION

1. Monitor your self-talk. Write down three negative and three positive things you say to yourself that affect how you feel about yourself. For each negative thought, write down an alternative thought to change the way you feel.

2. Identify at least two messages from your damaged image that you continue to say to yourself. Write down the truth, and counter those messages with the truth until they go away.

3. Identify some thoughts that qualify as "shame-talk." Counter them with "forgiveness talk."

4. In what areas is it most difficult to stand your ground against pressure from other people to conform? Develop a plan to let go of your need to please others. How will you do it?

5. What comes to mind when you read the following assessment? "You're not perfect. You're not going to be perfect. So accept your imperfections."

6. Which of your expectations about yourself are unreasonable? Write them down, and write more reasonable expectations for each one.

7. Who do you judge more harshly—yourself or others? How do the harsh judgments you make affect your relationships and your self-image? Can you extend the same grace to yourself and others?

8. How will you maintain your self-image when people project their images onto you through manipulation, judgment, false accusations, abuse, anger, demands, and blame?

9. What are your passions? What is your plan to identify and pursue them?

10. Name a few things you like about yourself. Name some things you don't like about yourself. How will you work on accepting the things you can't change and changing the things you can?

9

PROTECTING THE SELF-IMAGES OF

others

*ENCOURAGE ONE ANOTHER
AND BUILD EACH OTHER UP.*
—1 THESS. 5:11

6

PROTECTING THE SELF-IMAGES OF

others

ENCOURAGE ONE ANOTHER
AND BUILD EACH OTHER UP.
—1 THESS. 5:11

Developing an awareness of the things that affect our self-image naturally results in an increased focus on the importance of how we treat others. I experienced this while writing this book; I frequently reflected on the things that I do and don't do that impact the self-images of people in my life. I wish I could say I passed with flying colors, but I didn't. Like you, I'm growing and learning how to value not only myself but others too.

PROTECTING THE SELF-IMAGES OF CHILDREN

The self-images of children are vulnerable. Jesus had strong words for anyone who harmed a child by doing things that would cause him or her to sin, saying, "It would be better for him to have a large millstone hung around his neck and to be drowned in the depths of the sea" (Matt. 18:6). That's a strong statement, but it makes sense. We know that damaged self-images lead to low self-worth and low self-esteem, which result in bad choices later in life. Kids with low self-esteem get into more trouble and don't do as well as they might in school, and they become adults who have difficulties in relationships and with their life choices.

Anyone who is perceived as an authority figure to a child has an extra responsibility to treat that child in a way that guards his or her self-image. Parents have an especially important role, but so do other family members, teachers, coaches—anyone the child looks up to. Eph. 6:4 tells parents not to exasperate or provoke their children to wrath, but Jesus warned all of us not to provoke children to wrath (Matt. 18:6). Things that exasperate or provoke anger within a child are also things that harm his or her self-image. They include criticism, belittling, teasing, comparing, labeling, setting unattainable standards, unfair punishment, abuse, harshness, name-calling, raging, rejection, self-centeredness, abandonment, neglect, and projections.

All of us have done things in frustration, anger, or fatigue that we later regret. Before you take on the guilt of forever damaging the self-image of a child because you had a few weak moments, realize that what you do the most is what matters. As long as children have mostly positive input, they'll be OK. And it's never too late to start, so if you realize you haven't done what you would like to have done, begin today.

Let's look at ways you can protect the self-image of the children in your life. Many of them will apply directly to parents, but you can adapt the ideas to any relationship you have with a child.

Make Training a Priority

Discipline can build up or tear down. Discipline that's harsh, unfair, inconsistent, angry, rejecting, punitive, or abusive tears down the self-image of the child. When the purpose of discipline is to train, it builds the child up. We often focus on the punishment aspect of disciplining children, but the more important focus should be put on their training. Training takes place in every aspect of life and is done throughout the day each time you interact with children in any way (Deut. 6:6-9). Training means developing or guiding the habits and thoughts and helping the person become proficient through instruction and practice. God does this with us. His discipline is for our training rather than punishment, and in the end it produces good in our lives (Heb. 12:7-11).

Children with healthy self-images know who they are. Prov. 22:6 tells us to "train a child in the way he should go, and when he is old he will not turn from it." *Young's Literal Translation* puts it like this: "Give instruction to a youth about his way." We want to help children understand their way. What *is* their way? It's their natural bent, inborn personality, strengths, weaknesses, heart, soul, spirit, and purpose. Help them learn to capitalize on their strengths and adjust for their weaknesses. Help them understand the truth about God, the world, life, people, relationships, and themselves. Identify personality styles, traits, preferences, emotional strengths and weaknesses, areas of creativity, and styles of interacting. Help them find an identity that corresponds with the purpose for which God created them.

Punishment focuses on what a child does wrong and ignores what he or she does right. There's a place for punishment, of course, but it's a small part of the training process. Before I had children, I heard a woman talk about how she and her husband disciplined their children. An example she shared was giving one swat for every item out of place after telling them to clean their rooms. I knew those kids would grow up to be legalistic, rigid, fearful, and insecure.

An alternative to a system of rigid rules with specific imposed punishments is to discipline with logical consequences. Logical consequences recognize God's law of reaping what you sow (Gal. 6:7-8). Proverbs 28:19 gives this example: If you work your land, it will produce, and you'll have food, but if you don't, you'll be poor and hungry. Likewise, if children don't study, their grades will be lower. If they don't eat dinner, they'll be hungry until the next meal. When they're belligerent and difficult, they'll spend time alone until they can interact in a way that's respectful to everyone around them.

Renee was frustrated with her children's unwillingness to follow through with their chores and schoolwork. She nagged, yelled, took television time away, and threatened. Nothing worked. Finally, she decided to quietly allow natural consequences to take over. Renee told the kids once what the rules were and then said nothing more. Anyone who didn't do work at school had to do it at home before playing or watching television. Anyone who didn't pick up his or her toys lost them for an indefinite time. The kids had to come to her to show that chores and homework were done to get the OK to watch television or to play. Allowances were docked for undone chores to "pay" Renee for having to do them. Renee watched her kids become motivated and self-directed in a way she never had before, and she was much less frustrated.

Using logical consequences trains, teaches, and empowers kids. When they recognize that actions have consequences, they'll recognize that they can make different choices.

Discipline should guide but not shame the child. Jesus modeled this for us with His interaction with the woman caught in adultery brought to Him by the Pharisees (John 8:3-11). They wanted Jesus to condemn her; Jesus wanted her healed. He confronted the sin but let her know she could be forgiven and then changed.

Shame and labeling tell the child he or she is no good. Instead, label *behavior* as bad, and help the child gain insight about the action. Jimmy hit his little brother when he was frustrated. His mother, Molly, usually lost her temper, called him a brat, threatened to hit him back, and sent him to his room to be alone. Jimmy seemed to get even angrier after she punished him. Finally, she tried a different approach. Next time, she had him sit for 10 minutes, then talked to him about why he hit Johnny. Jimmy said he didn't like his brother because everyone loved him more and gave him better stuff. Molly empathized with his feelings and then talked to him about other things to do with those feelings instead of hitting.

Jimmy came up with several ideas. Afterward, Molly saw him make a better effort to control himself. When children do wrong, help them evaluate their choices. Say, "Do you think that was the wisest choice? What could you have done differently?" versus labeling their behavior and concluding that it comes from being willfully bad.

Focus on Internal Values

Because society focuses on external things—beauty, wealth, accomplishments, power, and abilities—it's easy to fall into that trap and reinforce those external values if you don't remind yourself to focus on internal character and qualities. That doesn't mean you ignore accomplishments, because we all need to feel good about what we do. Just don't equate *worth* with accomplishments.

It's important to compliment all children for their looks in some way. You can say, "You have pretty eyes," or "You have strong shoulders," or "You have nice hair." Tell a child that he or she is handsome, good-looking, pretty, or cute. After all, who's the judge of that really? What do you think God sees when He looks at our physical bodies? Be careful not to equate "ugly" with "bad" and "beautiful" with "good." Don't always tell stories that depict the weird-looking person as the bad guy. Amazingly, most of our fairy tales teach the unhealthy value that beauty means that you'll be loved: Sleeping Beauty, Rapunzel, and Cinderella all were rescued from their drudgery because of their beauty. The modern-day Shrek is a better example of character mattering more than looks. His true love chose to be an ugly ogre to be with him rather than a beautiful princess without him. Her father wasn't accepting of his daughter's choice to be with Shrek until it was revealed that he was really a frog himself masquerading as a king.

Value character. Tell stories, and point out incidents in people's lives that show the value of positive character traits and choices.

Compliment your children on their good character traits and virtuous acts. Helping your children see the strengths of their own character will help them understand their natural bent. It will also help them see themselves as they really are.

Value children by spending time with them. Nothing says love stronger to a child than an investment of your focused time and attention.

Teens really struggle with self-image. While it's important to assure them that there's more to life than external beauty via stylish clothes, shoes, and hairstyles, understand that in the teen world—especially for girls—not having those things can be devastating to their self-image.

Teach by Example

Modeling a good self-image is a powerful way to teach by example. Show that you're satisfied and contented with your life (Phil. 4:11-12), but continue to do the best you can in everything, knowing that you're working for the Lord and not to be approved by people (Col. 3:23). Don't be more focused on how you look than who you are as a person (1 Pet. 3:3-4). Don't criticize others because of their looks. Don't give preferential treatment to the rich, powerful, or beautiful (James 2:1-9). Don't constantly talk about your own appearance and criticize your own physical traits in front of your children. I admit I fail too often with this one. It pierces my conscience when I catch myself criticizing my looks. I vow to myself each time to be more careful. Criticizing yourself, especially for your physical traits that don't perpetuate the model of a perfect body or perfect looks, tells your children that they have to be perfect to be OK.

Keep a sense of humor and a light touch about life. Model optimism rather than pessimism. Mistakes aren't fatal—they're a necessary part of the learning process. Accept your mistakes. Offer grace to others. Show that you value other people and respect differences. Don't allow children to call other children names or put them down. Teach them to be sensitive to other people's weaknesses, and help them to learn to build others up.

Talk about yourself in a way that demonstrates a real and accurate self-image with high esteem and worth. Don't be embarrassed to admit when you do a good job. Accept compliments and praise when they're due. Exhibit true rather than false humility, and don't apologize for feeling confident and competent. Give the glory to God for His provision, but take the credit for your hard work and faithfulness. Find your purpose, and rejoice in living it.

Teach honesty and integrity. All of us feel good about ourselves when our insides match our outsides—when we're authentic. This is one way we obtain a real self-image. Honesty includes admitting when you're wrong and being willing to change. Model self-evaluation and self-responsibility. Don't blame your failures or your children's failures on others: teachers, friends, circumstances, yourself, God, or siblings. Take responsibility for your choices, and give your child the responsibility for his or hers.

Minimize materialism, and focus on the things that matter in your own life: eternity, spirituality, pleasing God, relationships, character, and doing what's right (Matt. 6:25-34). Don't reinforce materialism with your children by buying them everything they want or by living only for material gain and fun.

Instill Confidence and Competence

A person with a real self-image sees himself or herself honestly. Self-esteem and self-worth are closely related to a sense of adequacy and competence. People with low self-images and low self-esteem see themselves as inadequate and incompetent.

Kids who feel valued and competent have positive self-images. The valued part comes from knowing they're loved and accepted by people and God, and the competent part is what comes from being able to handle themselves and their lives. They feel empowered when they know they can control their lives with their actions. This doesn't mean they should be able to control the people in their environment—only themselves. The more stable a child's world is and the more control a child has, the more competent or adequate he or she feels. Instill confidence every way you can. Don't fix the child's work by going behind him or her and correcting what he or she does. If the bed isn't made perfectly or the floor isn't completely swept, accept it as good enough if it's reasonably done for the child's age and the child's attitude was good.

Competence is related to a good self-image. In fact, a child's self-image is closely linked to a sense of competence and resiliency. A child who believes he or she is capable of succeeding and meeting the challenges ahead will have high self-worth and self-esteem. You can relate this to your own life. When you feel completely out of control, inadequate, insecure, and uncertain, you feel badly about yourself. But if you feel competent, you feel more in control and better about yourself and your life. Imagine interviewing for a job for which you aren't qualified compared to going for an interview and knowing you're one of the most highly qualified applicants.

Develop your children's interests and talents. Find things they're good at so they can say, "I'm a good _____." It might be that they're able to draw, cook, build things, problem-solve, play a sport, or have an aptitude for a particular subject. Be proud of their individual abilities.

If your child has something about him or her that's different or that the other kids will tease or point out, help your child be prepared to deal with it. Help your child formulate a response or comeback so he or she won't be devastated when kids bring it up. Facing the truth and acknowledging it takes the power out of a criticism. If your child has a weakness or disability, take the upper hand. Learn about it. Help him or her understand it and make accommodation for it. It helps to know what one is dealing with. For example, for the child struggling in school, knowing that he or she has a learning disability that keeps the brain from processing information is easier to deal with than the overriding sense of inadequacy that comes from feeling that one is less than others or stupid.

Hank was born without a left arm below the elbow. He felt embarrassed and withdrew from the stares and teasing; he rarely defended himself. He wondered if God was punishing him. No one in his family talked to him about why it happened or how to deal with it. Hank's self-confidence could have been strengthened if he had been given help for dealing with his disability. It didn't have to destroy his self-image.

Strengthen your children's ability to articulate their beliefs and views by giving them permission to explain and defend opinions and preferences in the home. This gives them practice in standing firm in what they believe, an essential skill in today's world. I valued this tremendously with my three daughters. I erred on the side of letting them defend themselves too much rather than not enough, even if that meant I had to discuss more things with them. Today they're all strong, capable, and independent young women.

Strengthen and reinforce your children's right to set boundaries with other people, including friends, siblings, adults, and even you. Again, children need to know they're able to affect their environment. Having boundaries respected by you means they learn to expect that others will respect their wishes. People with good self-esteem want their boundaries respected. When they say no, they want the person to stop. In contrast, people with low self-esteem and self-worth don't expect their boundaries to be respected.

Offer Unconditional Acceptance

All of us long to be loved for who we are—inadequacies and all. Accept your child as he or she is, and love him or her in spite of imperfections and shortcomings. Don't compare your child to other siblings, other children, or yourself positively or negatively. Accept the child's natural "bent" even if it doesn't match your dream. The boy who isn't athletic can be devastated by the father who continues to dream of his son being the star of the football team. A daughter who is big and tomboyish instead of petite and feminine can have her self-esteem destroyed by parents who reject her for her lack of femininity. Don't tease children in their soft spots, especially for things they'll be teased about outside the home.

Sadly, Simon never felt as if he belonged to his family. He didn't look like them and was quiet and reserved rather than witty and gregarious. Everyone teased him and said he must have been switched in the nursery. Sometimes Simon believed he was, because he certainly didn't belong and didn't feel loved. In contrast, Simon's friend Eddie was also different than his brothers, more serious and brainy. But Eddie's family embraced his "different-ness" by calling him special and offering him opportunities to explore his interests. Eddie seemed to thrive on his uniqueness.

Make sure your expectations for your children fit them. Otherwise, they'll receive the message that "Who I really am is not OK." Appropriate expectations allow the child an opportunity to succeed so that competence and confidence will grow along with a real self-image. Keep expectations and feedback realistic. Don't try to build self-esteem and self-worth in your child on false compliments. If your child isn't good at something, don't pretend he or she is. The world will tell the truth, and you don't want children thinking they're great at something if they aren't. Don't talk about your child in front of other people as if he or she isn't in the room. And be careful about what you say.

Analyze your insecurities and broken dreams. Ask yourself, *Do I see my child as a reflection of me? Do I expect my child to achieve to boost my own self-esteem?* If so, work on your own self-image, and don't depend on your children to make you feel good about yourself.

Point out that God uses everything in our lives for our good and made each of us individually for His purpose. Our weaknesses can become our greatest assets, because God's "power is made perfect in weakness" (2 Cor. 12:9). Point out people who have overcome obstacles, physical handicaps, and negatives in their lives and built great lives. The ultimate giver of self-worth is God, who cared enough about each one of us that He sent His Son to die on the

Cross so we could live for eternity with Him. He knows us better than anyone else and still accepts us as His children (1 John 3:1).

PROTECTING THE SELF-IMAGES OF ADULTS

We also have a responsibility to protect the self-images of adults we encounter, whether they're family members, friends, acquaintances, or coworkers. The apostle Paul used the models of parents dealing with children to instruct us in how we should deal with others—including adults: "We were gentle among you, like a mother caring for her little children" (1 Thess. 2:7). "We dealt with each of you as a father deals with his own children, encouraging, comforting, and urging you to live lives worthy of God" (1 Thess. 2:11-12). Even when confrontation is necessary, it's to be done in a gentle and restorative way (Gal. 6:1). We can protect the self-image of adults in our lives by encouraging, accepting, and valuing them.

Encourage Them

"Encourage" means to impart courage or confidence and to admonish or urge forward. Self-esteem is directly related to one's confidence. Courage requires confidence. When Joshua was ready to go into the Promised Land after Moses' death, God encouraged him with these words: "Have I not commanded you? Be strong and courageous. Do not be terrified; do not be discouraged, for the LORD your God will be with you wherever you go" (Josh. 1:9). In other words, "Joshua, you can do it. You're a leader, and you'll succeed. Go, and I'll go with you." What a pep talk! Those powerful words continue to encourage us today.

We can encourage people by caring about them and walking through difficulties with them. We can "encourage the timid, help the weak, be patient with everyone" (1 Thess. 5:14). By letting others know we're there and understand, we can help turn their discouragement into courage. You may not know how to fix their problems or remove their pain, but you can validate them by accepting their feelings, opinions, beliefs, and values as legitimate.

Val's parents and husband repeatedly put her down and told her she wasn't capable of managing her life or deserving of good treatment. She believed their opinions about her and repeatedly put herself down. Her friend Kalie had a good self-image and didn't identify with Val's feelings, but she could see that Val was in a lot of pain. Kalie made it a point to spend time with Val and listen to her, and she also directed Val to some support groups that could help her.

There will also be times we must confront another person to avoid contributing to his or her false image. We "must put off falsehood and speak truthfully" to each other (Eph. 4:25). This is the side to encouragement called exhortation. Exhortation spurs the person on to do better (Heb. 10:24). We can do this in a way that imparts grace and hope rather than condemnation and shame (Gal. 6:1) but allows the person to bear the consequences of his or her choices (Gal. 6:7-8).

How we do it matters. "An honest answer is like a kiss on the lips" (Prov. 24:26), as long as it isn't given without concern for the person. Understand that people are naturally defensive when criticized. You must have a relationship with the person that entitles you to be direct, and what you have to say must not be delivered in a harsh or attacking way. It's also important to remember that some people are unwilling to take any correction or counsel (Prov. 12:15). These people will maintain their false images and refuse to self-evaluate. It takes wisdom to know when to speak and when to remain silent with these individuals (Prov. 26:4-5).

Accept Them

Each of us longs to be accepted and loved for who we are. "Accept" means to receive as adequate. When people allow themselves to be vulnerable, their fear is that they'll be rejected. The greatest thing you can do to protect the self-esteem and self-worth of those around you is to accept them as they are. This doesn't necessarily mean you'll want to be best friends with them. However, you can treat each person with the honor and respect that Jesus showed. Even the most quirky and strange among us has equal value in God's eyes, and, in fact, "the least" might actually have more! (Luke 9:48). God desires that you treat everyone the same and not show partiality, fulfilling the royal law of loving your neighbor as yourself (James 2:1-9). This isn't necessarily an easy thing to do, and it can often be accomplished only when God's love flows *through* you.

We're often the least accepting of our loved ones, yet most of us have been wounded the most by those who are closest to us. We can protect the self-images of our loved ones by speaking to them in ways that show we value them. And remember—maybe some of the things we're critical of are small things we can learn to overlook (1 Pet. 4:8).

Judging is the opposite of acceptance, and it condemns and labels. Recognize that people can be different than you and not be wrong; begin to accept those who are different without feeling inferior or superior to them (Rom. 14; 1 Cor. 10:23-30).

See people as Jesus did—with a heart of compassion and understanding. See them in light of their past and current situations to increase your empathy for them. Doris didn't understand Leslie's lack of motivation and her unwillingness to do something to improve her life. When Doris took the time to truly understand the depth of Leslie's battle with depression and the additional stress from her difficult marriage, she began to understand why it was hard for Leslie to make changes.

Alex found himself judging Kevin's lack of commitment in every area of his life. He quit one job after another and didn't follow through with his promises. Then Alex found out that Kevin's father had left when he was five years old. His mother battled alcoholism and threw Kevin out when he was sixteen. Kevin's self-esteem was so low that he didn't believe anyone liked him, so he withdrew when he felt unaccepted or unworthy.

"Empathy" means putting yourself in the other person's shoes to feel what it would be like to be him or her. It means you speak truth but offer grace and forgiveness. "The purposes of a man's heart are deep waters, but a man of understanding draws·them out" (Prov. 20:5). When you accept people as they are, you reflect back to them that they're valued. Not judging helps them to feel safe enough to share their vulnerabilities, pain, fears, hurts, and dreams with you.

Value Them

"Respect" means simply to honor and value. All of us are commanded to show respect to one another (1 Pet. 2:17). Look for ways and opportunities to say nice things. Most of us think positive things in our minds but fail to put those thoughts into words or action. Practice seeing past the outward physical characteristics; instead, train yourself to look inward at the soul.

Speak directly to people respectfully without guilt, manipulation, and a hidden agenda. Don't blame your stuff on them. Instead, take responsibility, and allow them to take responsibility for themselves. Deal with your own feelings so you won't project your feelings onto them. Examine your past, and identify the hot buttons that cause you to overreact in the present and do things that damage the self-images of others. Guard your tongue so you won't say things you later regret. Instead of your tongue crushing their spirits, let it bring life (Prov. 15:4).

Carly didn't understand why she screamed at her daughter, Leah, and berated her every time she didn't do well in her gymnastics routines, but it was clearly overboard, and she felt badly afterward. After some counseling, Carly understood that the kids had teased her relentlessly when she was a child because she wasn't well coordinated. When Leah didn't do well, it brought up the old feelings of shame and anger. She also feared that Leah would be ridiculed, as she was. Carly was able to stop the cycle when she understood its origin.

Invest some of your time and resources in those you value. Look people in the eye when you talk to them. Really listen. Be present and engaged in the moment, not distracted and distant. Help them discover who they are and what their passions are. Affirm their talents. Share yourself with them. Sharing your truth with them tells them you trust them and value them. When you're vulnerable with them, you make it safe for them to be real with you and accept their own imperfections.

IMPART A BLESSING

In Jewish homes it's customary to pass a blessing from the parents to the children and to pray blessings on people. A blessing imparts an identity, meaning, affirmation, and acceptance. In Hebrew, "to bless" means "to kneel." It bears the connotation of being in awe of someone. When we picture ourselves bowing our knees to God, it's out of our reverence and awareness of His greatness. When we bless others, it means to show them we value them.

God blessed Adam and Eve after creating them (Gen. 1:22). He blessed Abraham's descendants with His promise to make them a great nation and to bless those that blessed them and curse those that cursed them (Gen. 12:2-3). Jacob wrestled all night with God until God blessed him (Gen. 32:24-30). Israel (Jacob) blessed Joseph's sons and his own sons (Gen. 48:9-49:28). Jesus blessed the children brought to Him (Mark 10:13-16).

Each of us wants and needs God's blessing and the blessing of others. In fact, when we don't get that blessing, we may spend our lives doing things caused by low self-esteem and seek to receive the blessing from anyone who appears to be willing to give it to us. For some reason, when others don't esteem us, it's harder to esteem ourselves. When Esau found out that Jacob received his blessing from their father, he was despondent (Gen. 27:32-38).

When we protect the self-image of the adults and children in our lives, we reflect to them the grace and value God places on them. We help them to see themselves accurately, accept themselves as God has made them, and to become everything God intended them to be so they know they're valued and competent. We help them to have a real image. Bless the people in your life.

A SPECIAL BLESSING FOR YOU

And now I impart a blessing to you upon finishing this book: "May God be gracious to [you] and bless [you] and make his face shine upon [you]" (Ps. 67:1). "I pray that you, being rooted and established in love, may have power, together with all the saints, to grasp how wide and long and high and deep is the love of Christ, and to know this love that surpasses knowledge—that you may be filled to the measure of all the fullness of God. Now to him who is able to do immeasurably more than all [you] ask or imagine, according to his power that is at work within [you], to him be glory" (Eph. 3:17-21). Amen.

QUESTIONS FOR REFLECTION

1. What is your philosophy regarding disciplining children?

2. Why do you think using logical consequences boosts a child's self-esteem and self-worth? How do you allow both children and adults in your life to bear the consequences of their own actions?

3. What values do you model by your priorities, words, actions, values, choices, and beliefs? Do you focus more on internal or external things (character versus physical looks and material things)?

4. Reflect on your self-image and the things you say about yourself. What are you communicating to others?

5. How are you helping people in your life become more competent and confident?

6. How do you show acceptance and nonacceptance of people in your life?

7. How do you encourage people in your life? What are some of the things you do that discourage them?

8. How do you value people in your life? What things do you do that show you don't value, honor, and respect them?

9. Did you receive a blessing from your parents? Who blesses you today? How do you bless others?

10. Write two things you plan to change that will help you do better at protecting the self-image of people in your life.

About the Author

KARLA DOWNING

is an author, counselor, speaker, and Twelve Step recovery program leader with a passion to help people understand and apply the Bible in practical and life-changing ways that set them free from the chains of dysfunction, misunderstanding, and emotional pain. Her passion also includes helping ministry leaders and lay counselors reach out more effectively to those in difficult relationships. Her first book, *10 Lifesaving Principles for Women in Difficult Marriages,* was a 2004 ECPA Gold Medallion finalist. Her second book, *When Love Hurts: 10 Principles to Transform Difficult Relationships,* applies the same principles to all relationships. Karla has also written articles for women's ministry leaders for LifeWay International including two downloadable resources titled *Women Reaching Women in Crisis: Drug/Alcohol Dependency* and *Women Reaching Women in Crisis: Domestic Violence/Abuse.* Karla has a Master of Arts degree in marriage and family therapy. She lives in southern California with her husband and three daughters.

An ECPA Gold Medallion Finalist

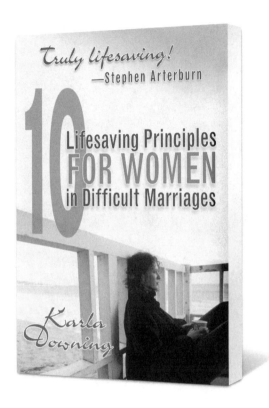

Regardless of the specific problems in your marriage, this book will help you find peace and confidence.

Karla Downing gives you the principles needed to overcome your sense of powerlessness and ultimately improve your life.

10 Lifesaving Principles for Women in Difficult Marriages
By Karla Downing
ISBN-13: 978-0-8341-2050-1

BEACON HILL PRESS
OF KANSAS CITY

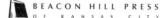

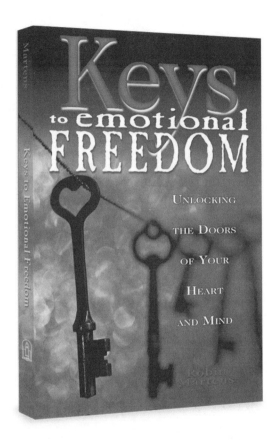

Keys to Emotional Freedom offers specific advice,
encouraging examples, relevant scripture, and practical
steps to help you begin the habit of leaving emotional
baggage at the foot of the cross. Learn to rest in
the joy and peace of emotional freedom.

Keys to Emotional Freedom

Unlocking the Doors of Your Heart and Mind

By Robin Martens

ISBN-13: 978-0-8341-2174-4

BEACON HILL PRESS
OF KANSAS CITY